THE INTIMACY YOU DESIRE

the
Intimacy
You
Desire

GROWING
IN LOVE WITH
GOD THROUGH
THE SPIRITUAL
EXERCISES OF
SAINT IGNATIUS

TOM ELLIOTT

TWENTY-THIRD
PUBLICATIONS
twentythirdpublications.com

TWENTY-THIRD PUBLICATIONS
One Montauk Avenue, Suite 200
New London, CT 06320
(860) 437-3012 or (800) 321-0411
www.twentythirdpublications.com

ISBN: 978-1-62785-353-8
Library of Congress Control Number: 2017960975
Printed in the U.S.A.

 A division of Bayard, Inc.

Contents

Introduction

New Orleans is known for many things; seminary is not one of them. Yet the Big Easy is where I spent four years of graduate school studying to be a priest. I heard and saw many new things during my four years at Notre Dame Seminary. For example, I heard the word "convocation" for the first time, which I assumed was just a fancy word for "lecture." The priest who was in charge of the seminary would call all of us together for monthly convocations. Most of these were uneventful and relatively uninformative, but I'll never forget the evening he lectured us about prayer.

After we gathered in the small room, the rector of the seminary addressed us, saying, "Gentlemen, if you're struggling with your academics, we will get you a tutor, but if you're not spending an hour a day in personal prayer, then you need to get out." He emphatically and clearly expressed that prayer was more important than good grades. I took his words to heart and began spending an hour each morning in personal prayer.

I woke up every day at 5 AM and headed to the chapel, stopping briefly at the cafeteria for a cup of coffee. I sleepily shuffled into the seminary chapel, my cup of java in one hand and my Bible in the other. Sitting down on one of the seemingly ancient wooden pews, I was enveloped in quiet darkness. After reading Scripture for a few minutes and sipping my coffee, I found myself bored and distracted, wondering what I was supposed to do next. Sometimes, I grabbed my rosary hoping to fill up the hour; other mornings, I played "Bible roulette," randomly opening the word of God and hoping it would be exactly what I wanted to hear. Regardless of the method I used for prayer each morning, the bottom line was simple: I didn't know how to pray. I simply tried to get through the sixty minutes so that I could get on with my day. I desired intimacy with God but wasn't sure what that really looked like or how to reach it. I felt disconnected from God.

After being ordained a priest in June 1999, I continued to struggle with personal prayer. I quickly fell into a pattern of "binge praying," avoiding prayer for several days and then binging for a few hours. During that time, my spiritual director, whom I met with each month, frequently questioned me about my prayer time. His concern was always expressed in a very particular, albeit peculiar, question, "Are you getting to happy hour every day?" "Happy hour" was his unique phrase for spending an hour in prayer. The phrase was cute and catchy—until we were in a crowded restaurant (in our priestly attire), surrounded by people who were already skeptical of priests. At such times, his loud question drew looks of shock and disgust from bystanders.

Sadly, month after month my answer to his question was, "Not every day." By this I meant that I was praying once every few days, still unsure of what in the world I was supposed to be doing for an hour. This continued for the first few years of my priesthood until, one day, a Protestant woman walked into my office and told me that she was being plagued by demons. Meeting her changed my prayer life in an unexpected way.

I'll never forget the day she sat across the desk from me, looking timid and nervous. Undoubtedly, this was the first time she had ever visited a Catholic priest, and she didn't know what to expect. All she knew was that she had reached out for help to countless others, and no one had been able to relieve her of the demons. After she shared her story with me, I scheduled a time to bless her house, since that is where most of the spiritual attacks had occurred. The house blessing, however, did not help.

My next step was to contact the exorcist for our diocese. He generously talked with me about the woman's situation and offered a couple of simple suggestions; however, his suggestions, like the house blessing, failed to help her. Frustrated, I contacted a religious community in Nebraska that was known for their knowledge of spiritual warfare. By the time I received their materials in the mail, I had been regularly meeting with the woman for more than a year.

The box they sent was filled with numerous books, pamphlets, and audiotapes. Rather than information about spiritual warfare, the majority of the materials was about spiritual formation. Unfamiliar with the concept, I thoroughly studied all of the materials and, instead of simply learning a technique to solve the woman's demonic troubles, I learned how to pray. While I was never able to help the woman find peace, I discovered within myself a deep desire for intimacy with God.

Prayer became more and more regular. It grew from sporadic to consistent, and from a few minutes a day to a nonnegotiable hour every day. During prayer, I heard God speak to me in new and meaningful ways. As I grew in my relationship with God, I found myself excited each morning to get up and go to my prayer chair to spend time with him. I felt a deep sense that something important was happening in my life and in my relationship with God, but I really wasn't sure how it was happening. Something in the spiritual formation materials seemed to have healed my struggles with prayer and helped me feel more connected to God, but I didn't have a sense of exactly what had helped, at least not yet.

Shortly after my holy hour became a nonnegotiable experience every morning, Bishop Sartain offered me the opportunity to begin a three-year training program in spiritual direction. The training included extensive study of a retreat manual written by Saint Ignatius of Loyola known as the *Spiritual Exercises*. I wasn't familiar with Ignatius' writing, but as we studied it I realized the spiritual formation material that had helped me with my prayer was based on Ignatius' writing. I could see more specifically *how* the formation materials had helped me as I learned that the *Spiritual Exercises* reveal and encourage deepening levels of relationship with God and offer tools for relational prayer, leading to the apex of the *Exercises*—mutuality with God. Despite no longer being a priest, those tools continue to be essential to my intimacy with God.

My reason for writing *The Intimacy You Desire* is to help you discover the same thing—the intimacy you desire with God. You will be offered an opportunity to get to know Ignatius, read about the deepening levels of intimacy that he offers in the *Spiritual Exercises*, grapple with the scandalously intimate reality of God's desire for mutual love with us, and learn new ways to experience profoundly relational personal prayer. Words like intimate, mutual, and relational will become interchangeable descriptions of your personal prayer and relationship with God!

REFLECTION QUESTIONS

I conclude each chapter in this book with reflection questions. These can be used during your personal prayer time or as spiritual formation in a small group. If you use them in a group, I recommend covering one chapter a week, with members of the group reading it individually and reflecting on the questions during personal prayer time. Then, at the group meetings each week, members can share their answers with one another.

1. What are the most significant moments in your life—emotionally, vocationally, and spiritually?

2. When was your most significant encounter with God? How did it change you?

3. When in your life did you feel like your prayer life was the most fruitful? Why?

4. When in your life did you experience profound dryness in your personal prayer time? How did you respond to the dryness?

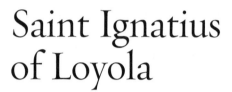

CHAPTER ONE

Saint Ignatius of Loyola

I knew very little about Saint Ignatius of Loyola when I started the spiritual direction training program in 2003. The program, led by the Institute for Priestly Formation, helped me develop my personal prayer life, taught me the ministry of spiritual direction, and introduced me to one of the most significant people in my life today, Ignatius. There are countless amazing books written about the life and teachings of Saint Ignatius of Loyola, including his autobiography; therefore, I will not offer a complete survey of Ignatius's life in this book.[1] Instead, I

---

1   Ignatius. *A Pilgrim's Journey: The Autobiography of Ignatius of Loyola*. Trans. Joseph N. Tylenda. Ignatius Press, 1991.

will offer a brief snapshot of his life, and then we'll look at the deepening intimacy he invites us to experience with God in and through the *Spiritual Exercises*.

Ignatius was born in 1491 at his family's castle of Loyola in Spain. As a young man, he was much like other men of his time, both in vice and in virtue. Ignatius enjoyed the common vanities of his day, including lofty dreams of winning glory and being famous. In order to accomplish those dreams, Ignatius entered the army in 1517. During a battle with the French in 1521, he was injured by a cannonball and was taken to the castle of Loyola to recuperate. In order to pass the time during his seven months there, Ignatius' sister-in-law offered the two books that were kept in the house—*Life of Christ* by Ludolph Saxony and *Lives of the Saints* by Jacobus de Voragine. These books helped turn his mind from fantasies of worldly chivalry and fame to hopes of spiritual greatness. Ignatius began to understand his life and purpose differently, and by the end of his recovery an interior spiritual conversion had begun.

In the years following his recovery and conversion, Ignatius journeyed to numerous countries, spending a tremendous amount of time praying and serving the poor. In his *Autobiography*, Ignatius describes some of the significant religious experiences he had during that time. One such mystical moment, which took place on the steps of a monastery, allowed Ignatius to experience the mutuality and unity of the Holy Trinity. Ignatius described the moment, writing in the third person: "His understanding began to be elevated so that he saw the Most Holy Trinity in the form of three keys. This brought on so many tears and so much sobbing that he could not control himself..."[2] These "keys," or *teclas* in Spanish, probably signify a musical chord, which is three notes, but one harmonious sound—a beautiful image of the Trinity and of unity. More than just an image, Ignatius' prayer was an experience of the heart, an interior movement of God that permanently emblazoned him with knowledge of God's unity and love.

In another mystical experience, Ignatius described something white, which emitted rays of light. According to what Ignatius wrote at the end of the *Spiritual Exercises*, this spiritual experience illustrated the generosity of God, who freely shares rays of himself—graces, virtues, and created gifts. Ignatius came to understand this generosity as an important part of the mutual intimacy that we desire—the sharing of goods and self.

These and other religious experiences humbly reminded Ignatius that God desires to share his goods and his very self with all of us. Ignatius never restricted such experiences to himself; rather, he believed that God desired to communicate in similar intimate ways with everyone. This belief found clear expression in the *Spiritual Exercises*, which he worked on from 1522 until 1540.

The sincerity and spirituality that flowed out of Ignatius and his writings drew followers to him, and they began to form a community. In 1534 Ignatius and some of his companions took vows to work for others and to live in poverty, and in 1537 they were ordained priests and moved toward founding a new religious order, the Society of Jesus.

As you might imagine, the founding members of the Society

2   Ignatius. pp. 37-39.

of Jesus elected Ignatius as the first superior general. Despite the fact that he turned down the election a couple of times, the Holy Spirit prevailed, and Ignatius accepted the position toward the end of 1540. For the next fifteen years, he focused his time and energy on administrative work for the Society while living in Rome.

In 2010, I had the privilege of visiting the house of the Gesù in Rome, where Ignatius lived and worked. While the house is not one of the popular pilgrimage sites in Rome, it is a great stop for those who love Ignatius. For example, a brief tour of the house reveals some relics of Ignatius' presence and work there, such as his desk, prayer books, one of the first editions of the *Spiritual Exercises*, and some clothes. In the corridor, there is also a painting of Saint Ignatius playing billiards with the viceroy of Spain. Legend has it that Ignatius told the viceroy that no game of pool was complete without a bet and proposed that the loser would have to do anything the winner wanted him to do for thirty days. Ignatius won, of course, and required the viceroy to go through the thirty-day retreat of the *Exercises*!

Undoubtedly, the greatest treasure Ignatius left us is the *Spiritual Exercises*. For more than four hundred fifty years, countless men and women—lay and religious, Catholic and non-Catholic—have been led through the *Exercises* either in a thirty-day silent retreat (four "Weeks") or in the course of their normal daily lives. In the last few decades a growing interest and appreciation for the *Exercises* has developed, quite possibly because they offer us a glimpse of the intimacy with God that we so deeply desire.

REFLECTION QUESTIONS

1. What events in your life have caused you to be more aware of God?

2. What sins have hindered your acceptance of God's love?

3. What gifts and blessings have helped you to accept God's love?

4. What books, movies, songs, etc., have been instrumental in your spiritual journey?

5. Who are the people who have played the most significant role in your relationship with God? Why?

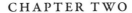

CHAPTER TWO

Intimacy in the Spiritual Exercises

Healthy relationships are not haphazard, but rather they involve our deliberate and conscious participation. Such active participation allows us to name and understand the nuances of relationships and have a sense of whether or not they're growing. As you might imagine, this is not always easy! For example, one of my directees shared with me his frustration with a friend of his. As he shared the story of their relationship, he realized that it was no longer a *friendship*, but a *ministry*. He described how all of the conversations with this presumed friend were always one-sided; there wasn't mutual sharing but only the other person's neediness.

Rather than being life-giving, the relationship was life-draining.

Through prayer and spiritual direction this man was able to accept that the relationship was a ministry instead of a friendship, which helped him to be more fully present to the other person without feeling used. It also helped him establish new boundaries that were healthy for ministry, rather than the boundaries typically expected in a friendship. Simply understanding the essence of the relationship created a place of great freedom and peace for him.

Naming and understanding our relationships can provide us with tremendous freedom, focus, peace, and energy. This is not only true in our human relationships, but also in our relationship with God, which can be understood and experienced in countless different ways, as we see in the gospels. People understood their relationship with Christ in ways that were antagonistic, needy, friendly, curious, close, mutual, deceitful, manipulative, or generous. They related to Jesus as if he was their benefactor, physician, companion, or friend, to name a few. Understanding and naming our relationship with God lets us savor and appreciate the nuances of that relationship, as well as grow in a desire for deeper intimacy.

The apex of relationship with God presented by Saint Ignatius of Loyola in the *Spiritual Exercises* is mutuality. Such intimacy does not happen magically or instantaneously but develops and deepens over time. The *Exercises* invite retreatants into that deepening relationship as each "Week," or part, of the retreat offers a particular level of relationship with God. While Ignatius does not specifically name these levels of relationship, I found myself naming them as I finished the *Exercises*. As I entered into the mutuality of Week Four found in the "Contemplation to Attain

Divine Love," I realized that the various graces, or spiritual gifts, that Ignatius invites retreatants to pray for in each of the Weeks were precisely leading them through levels, or depths, of intimacy.

In this chapter, I present the levels of relationship with God found in each of the four Weeks, as well as a brief overview of the meditations that Ignatius offers us as a way of savoring that relationship. At the risk of oversimplifying the complexities of our relationship with God, I will also share the story of a couple, Rick and Megan, whose love is a beautiful illustration of the ever-deepening movement of love we experience with God in the *Exercises*.

Principle and Foundation

Ignatius believed that our spiritual journey starts with an experience of falling in love with God, which he describes in the beginning of *Spiritual Exercises* as a "Principle and Foundation" experience. This makes practical sense to most of us because we've experienced how falling in love often begins our relationships with others. That was Rick's experience as he shared with me the first time he met Megan. Even though it was almost forty years ago, he seemed to remember it like it was yesterday. He explained how he had gotten off of work at the grocery store and headed to a favorite restaurant with two friends. As he described the restaurant, I told Rick it sounded more like a bar. He quickly told me that falling in love with a woman at a bar would be too cliché and, therefore, it was a restaurant that staged the grand moment when a young woman named Megan became his "pearl of great price."[3] Rick explained to me that the moment he saw her, he fell madly in love.

---

3   Matthew 13:44–46.

That brief encounter with Megan changed Rick's life forever. He wanted to spend more time with her. He desired to be a better man, someone of whom she would be proud. As months of dating unfolded, Rick noticed that he was less selfish and more generous and thoughtful. Being surprised by love began bearing the fruit of love. This is precisely what the "Principle and Foundation" experience of God is like—it's a falling in love that begins to change us. We begin questioning our motives and desires, reprioritizing them in light of the love we've experienced.

The grace, or spiritual gift, that Ignatius invites us to pray for during this particular time in our relationship with God is to know God's unconditional love for us. Like Rick's love for Megan, our experience of God's love moves beyond mere head-knowledge and pierces our hearts in a life-changing way. We see God, others, and ourselves with a fresh set of eyes and we desire to learn and experience more. We finally begin to realize what we want, what we truly desire!

The "Principle and Foundation" introduction to the *Spiritual Exercises* is very short, just a few paragraphs, however, it is an enormous wellspring of material for our prayer and reflection. My favorite translation of it is a paraphrase by David Fleming, which reads—

God who loves us creates us
and wants to share life with us forever.
Our love response takes shape
in our praise and honor and service of the God of our life.

All the things in this world are also created
    because of God's love

and they become a context of gifts,
presented to us so that we can know God more easily
and make a return of love more readily.

As a result, we show reverence for all the gifts of creation
and collaborate with God in using them
so that by being good stewards
we develop as loving persons in our care of God's world
 and its development.

But if we abuse any of these gifts of creation or,
on the contrary, take them as the center of our lives,
we break our relationship with God
and hinder our growth as loving persons.

In everyday life, then, we must hold ourselves in balance
before all created gifts insofar as we have a choice
and are not bound by some responsibility.

We should not fix our desires on health or sickness,
wealth or poverty, success or failure, a long life or a short one.
For everything has the potential of calling forth in us
a more loving response to our life forever with God.
Our only desire and our one choice should be this:
I want and I choose what better leads to God's deepening life
 in me.[4]

---

4 Fleming, David. *Draw Me into Your Friendship*. Institute for Advanced Jesuit Studies, 2016, p. 27.

Without actually using the word "mutuality," the "Principle and Foundation" clearly describes our relationship with God as mutual. This begins with Ignatius defining the purpose of life as *relationship* with God by writing, "God who loves us creates us and wants to share life with us forever." Notice that the goal is not to get to a place, such as heaven. Nor is the goal to accomplish holy things, such as growing in virtue, or appeasing a demanding God. Instead, the goal is *being with a Person*—God. To be with God means to *know* God; therefore, Ignatius is not inviting us to know *about* God, but rather to "know God more easily."

Many Christians today know *about* God or, more accurately, know about religion, and can vehemently and precisely defend their religious beliefs. However, they have yet to experience the intimate knowing *of* God and being known *by* God. Some of them have evidently read about other people's relationships with God and have familiarized themselves with the language of mutual love, but they have not made the challenging journey into intimacy with God.

When people's prayer lives are founded on knowing *about* God rather than mutuality *with* God, their spirituality comes out as pietism and religiosity. They try to talk about a path they haven't yet walked and, therefore, must minimize faith to "having correct ideas about things, or...as a moral worthiness contest to win entrance into the next world."[5] Such people stand in stark contrast to those who have actually made the long journey, whether through the *Exercises* or through other forms of prayer.

In addition to the summons found in the first sentence,

---

5   Rohr, Richard. "Inertia Resists Change." *The Naked Now*. Crossroad Publishing Company, 2009.

there are other invitations into intimacy and mutuality in the "Principle and Foundation." For example, Ignatius reminds us that our response to God's love "takes shape in our praise and honor and service of the God of our life" and God's gifts allow us to "make a return of love more readily." This mutual sharing of goods and, even more importantly, this mutual sharing of *selves* is the apex of intimacy. This is what God desires with us!

The "Principle and Foundation" reminds us of the power of authentic love—it refocuses our lives, purifies our desires, and deepens our sense of self and others. This was precisely what Rick was talking about when he explained how falling in love with Megan made him desire to be a better man. He realized that he desired more than a bachelor lifestyle. He knew that he needed to be lovingly accepted and "rescued" by Megan precisely in his woundedness, pride, control, and selfishness. This is what the "Principle and Foundation" experience of God's love offers. Our awareness of our need to be rescued then leads us into the grace of Week One of the *Exercises*.

Week One

When I began doing pastoral counseling years ago, I never would have guessed that the number one demographic walking through my office door would be middle-aged, married women who were angry at their husbands for not being actively engaged with their faith. Their stories were all very similar. They shared with me how, while dating years ago, their husbands explained to them that they were not into the whole "church thing." The women acknowledged that fact, even though faith was important to them. Yet, after years of marriage, the women were now resentful of their husbands' lack of spirituality. When I pointed out to the women that their husbands had forewarned them of their disinterest in religion, the women all responded with the exact same words, "I thought he would change."

Marriage counselors frequently remind us that authentic love does not hold unfounded hope that the other will change. Instead, it accepts the other in a healthy form of "rescuing." In other words, authentic love doesn't demand change as much as it rescues us *in* our imperfection through radical acceptance. Rick experienced something similar in his relationship with Megan. Despite the fact that his love for her caused him to want to be a better man, Rick knew he came up short; he still had faults, wounds, and sins. Yet Megan accepted him as he was and loved him despite his imperfections. Only in such radical acceptance can we experience being rescued *in* our brokenness, not necessarily *from* our brokenness. This is an important truth and experience in Week One of the *Exercises*. As such, the grace that Ignatius invites us to pray for is to see ourselves as loved sinners, falling short of what God intends yet cherished beyond imagining.

Through the meditations found in Week One, we are invited to understand ourselves better, name our wounds, and accept God's love despite our sinfulness. Ignatius begins by inviting us to meditate on the history of creation. In doing so, we are challenged to take off our spiritual blinders and view the reality of sin in the world and in our lives, including our role in it. This is not an easy meditation! Our egos hate this level of honesty and transparency. We would much rather stay in our constructed "realities" where everyone else is to blame for the brokenness and hurt in our lives and our world. We tend to be very resistant to this level of honesty regarding our darkness.

In Week One we experience a freedom to admit that the "god"

we have worshipped is often nothing more than a projection of our own ego and our "theology" is often nothing more than our own superficial wants. Authentic love is the only thing powerful enough to allow us to be that honest. We begin to see more clearly how we have been trapped by sin, and we experience a freedom to take responsibility for it. We find ourselves growing in self-awareness and God-awareness.

As this particular Week of the *Exercises* continues, the focus shifts from introspection to God. This is necessary since we can only take an honest look at our sinfulness and the evil in the world in light of God's love and mercy. Otherwise, looking at our sinfulness would quickly lead to self-hate and scrupulosity. Without the love found in the cross of Christ, our sinfulness would destroy us in condemnation. Through God's unconditional love, however, we can let the false self of our brokenness and darkness be overwhelmed by Light.

All of this is to simply say that, in Week One, we experience God as our rescuer; he meets us and saves us precisely in our brokenness and sinfulness. This rescuing, as I mentioned earlier, is not so much our being rescued *from* sin, as if sinlessness was the goal of life, but that we are rescued *in* our sin, which allows us to know that we are not alone and that we are of great value. That wonderful quote from Saint Paul comes to mind—"God proves his love for us in that while we were still sinners Christ died for us" (Romans 5:8). When we could not save ourselves, Love rescued us!

George Aschenbrenner, a Jesuit priest and author, offers a great image of the grace and rescue of Week One. He invites us to imagine that we are in a house that has caught fire. In our attempt to escape the house, we fall and injure ourselves. As the fire spreads, we realize that we must gather all of our strength and crawl out of the blaze. However, despite our best efforts, we are unable to move. As the fire quickly encircles us and smoke begins to burn our lungs, an important realization surfaces—we are unable to save ourselves, and we are going to die. We resign ourselves to that overwhelming truth. We accept it. Then, through the scorching flames, we see a man walking toward us. He lovingly scoops us up and carries us to safety. We have been rescued not by our own power, willfulness, or resourcefulness, but by Another. Our hearts are so filled with gratitude that we desire to follow our rescuer and become his companion.

Like Megan's love for Rick, God's love rescues us, which is fundamentally different from trying to fix us or change us. Such authentic love and acceptance is unbelievably freeing. This freedom is necessary if we are going to let our relationship with God deepen further, from rescuer to companion.

Week Two

Having completed Week One of the *Spiritual Exercises*, we find ourselves focusing less on ourselves and more on God and others. We have experienced true sorrow for our sins and God's overwhelming mercy. We find our relationship with God is moving from that of being rescued to being his companion. Often at this stage of the *Exercises* we have to confront our fear of losing ourselves. This is true not only in our relationship with God, but also in our relationships with others. Rick experienced this when he and Megan started dating.

While he desired to "grow up and become a man," Rick struggled to embody the kindness, thoughtfulness, and generosity that Megan desired and deserved. He was used to a bachelor lifestyle in which he did whatever he wanted and had no one to be concerned about except himself. His love for Megan, though, overpowered his fear of losing his autonomy and independence. Slowly, he became less and less preoccupied with himself and more interested in getting to know Megan. He wanted to spend as much time with her as possible. He wanted to know everything about her! These wants are very similar to the ones that lead us into Week Two of the *Exercises*. Having fallen in love and been rescued (i.e., accepted despite our failings), we desire to know our rescuer, Jesus, more intimately and to be more heroic and selfless as a response to his love.

The grace, or spiritual gift, that Ignatius invites us to pray for in Week Two is to gain an intimate knowledge of Christ, so as to love him more deeply and follow him more faithfully. As we pray for this grace, we find ourselves desiring to read the gospels and meditate on what Jesus said and did. We deeply desire to get to know him! This is a time of deliberately being a disciple of Christ; by learning from the Rabbi, we are molded and shaped into his image and likeness.

The first meditation in Week Two is titled, "The Kingdom Exercise." In this meditation, Ignatius invites us to reflect on how we would respond to a king's invitation to serve him. The goal of this meditation is to help us recognize and accept that our Companion desires for us to share in his mission and to zealously respond to his call. There is great humility in the truth that God desires for us to *share* his mission. He is not asking us to get out of his way so that he can work, nor is he demanding that we do this or that. Instead, we are invited to companion with him in a shared mission just as the Apostles companioned with Christ.

Next, Ignatius invites us to reflect on various aspects of Jesus' incarnation, birth, and hidden life in Nazareth. Using a style of prayer known as "imaginative prayer," we draw near to Jesus and grow in intimacy with him by letting ourselves become participants in the gospel stories. We find ourselves becoming like Jesus in noticeable ways, just as we often pick up the idiosyncrasies and characteristics of those with whom we frequently hang around.

Then, moving from these Scripture meditations back to a meditation that Ignatius himself wrote, he invites us to reflect on the "Two Standards." Here, the word "standard" is used by Ignatius to mean "banner" or "flag," such as a soldier would carry into battle. During this meditation, we are invited to grow in our awareness of how Christ operates and how Satan operates in our lives; each has his own standard, or banner. This meditation is not so much about choosing Christ (we've already done that), but about refining how we examine our lives, noticing how we can more fully follow Christ and more deliberately avoid Satan's traps. Something very similar happens in most human companionships.

Rick noticed that the more he and Megan dated, the more he wanted to do things that pleased her. In the beginning of their relationship, he looked for big ways to impress her but, after several months, he found himself looking for simpler ways, such as cooking her favorite meal and loading the dishwasher the way she preferred. This is precisely the subtlety of love that develops in Week Two of the *Exercises*. We learn the preferences and characteristics of Christ and we serve him—follow his standard—in those ways. This naturally leads us to Ignatius' next meditation where we reflect on the three different ways a person could choose to live his or her life.

In the meditation "The Three Classes of Persons," Ignatius explains how every Christian lives in one of three ways—completely heedless of God or others, hopeful that God will approve all that we choose to do, or simply for God. I would dare to say that many of us have spent a large portion of our lives as the first class of persons. I would even go so far as to say that most Christians in the world never move beyond the second class. The third class is a radical and unselfish form of love—to live wholly for the Other. This is precisely where companionship with Christ is leading us.

After this meditation, we are invited to go back to the gospel stories of Christ's life and ministry. Ignatius challenges us to get to know Christ more intimately, not just knowing *about* him but, through imaginative prayer, *encountering* him. George Aschenbrenner describes this intimate knowing by writing, "To learn the person is to enter that person's heart....In the Second Week, contemplation will help you to learn Jesus, to enter the tabernacle of his heart, to encounter him in an intimate and zealous faith."[6] With the same zeal that led Rick to learn more about Megan, we find ourselves going back to the gospel narratives over and over, spending time with Christ and getting to know him.

Maybe because of a fascination with the number three, Ignatius then invites retreatants to reflect on the "Three Degrees of Humility." In essence, Ignatius describes three degrees of *love* more so than *humility* when he explains that we should grow from 1) loving God so much that we would not want to break any of his commandments or laws, to 2) loving God so much that we desire to be sensitive to even the slightest desires of his heart and to choose to act on them, to 3) loving God so much that we become inclined to choose everything the world hates. Once again, I think most of us spend the majority of our lives in the first degree of humility with most Christians never moving past the second. The

---

6   Aschenbrenner, George. *Stretched for Greater Glory.* Loyola Press, 2004, pp. 79-80.

third degree describes a radical form of intimacy that requires us to truly know Christ's heart and to want to imitate him.

While Ignatius' third degree of humility might be a bit confusing at first, it begins to make sense in light of the grace we're praying for in Week Two—to gain an intimate knowledge of Christ so as to love him more deeply and follow him more faithfully. As we know, Jesus constantly turns our view of life upside down. For example, the things that the world loves, Jesus hated. So, the third degree of humility is not so much about being in opposition to the world but about being a reflection of Christ's disposition. For example, we might have begun the *Exercises* thinking more like the world, such as, "Blessed are the rich and successful." But, having hung out with Christ through our meditations on the gospel stories, we have begun taking on his characteristics and values to the point that we understand and believe such things as, "Blessed are the poor" (Luke 6:20b).

Having led us to being more intimately conformed to Christ, Ignatius ends Week Two of the *Exercises* with some suggestions and meditations regarding discerning one's "way of life." These suggestions and meditations can be applied to other important decisions in our lives, not just our vocational discernment. Keeping with his pragmatic style, Ignatius offers distinct methods and meditations to guide us through discerning God's will in various situations. While not everyone going through the *Exercises* is discerning a specific question, Ignatius' suggestions are helpful spiritual tools for everyone to learn.

For those who have journeyed with Christ as his companion and grown in love for him through Week Two, a desire to take the relationship to the next level has grown. We find ourselves so in love with Christ that we are willing to journey anywhere with him, even into suffering. Rick experienced something very similar when Megan's sister suddenly died. While it was a difficult and painful experience, it permanently transformed their relationship.

Week Three

Rick and Megan had only been dating for a little over a year when Megan's sister died in a car accident. Being with Megan in her grief solidified their relationship. As days turned into weeks following the accident, Megan began to realize that Rick loved her in good times and in bad. She knew that if Rick could be present with her in deep suffering, his love was authentic. Rick had become for Megan more than just a companion and friend; she knew that he was her best friend and she could wholeheartedly trust him to be by her side through anything. This is precisely the gift and relationship we discover in Week Three of the *Exercises*. The graces of Week Two prepare us for that new depth of relationship.

We know we are ready to move from Week Two to Week Three when we notice several important changes happening in our lives, such as loving in a new way. For example, our old way of loving might have been similar to what author Mary Beth Bonacci calls "pizza love," where we minimize love to what the object of our affection can do for us. "I love pizza," we say. Yet what we mean is, "I love what pizza does for me!"[7] Similarly, our old way of loving others might have been rooted in selfishness regarding what they could do for us. Our new way of loving, however, might be much more radical and Christlike, including a willingness to "lay down one's life for one's friends" (John 15:13).

---

7 Bonacci, Mary Beth. *Real Love*. Ignatius Press, 2012, p. 22.

Also, having journeyed through Week Two, we tend to look past superficial things and desire to live more deeply; we are more patient, more discerning, more contemplative, and more trusting. In short, we have become more like Christ. Men and women who are going through the *Exercises* will sense a readiness to move from Week Two to Week Three when they experience an ever-increasing willingness to be present with Christ even in his suffering, a desire to generously serve, and a sense of being an apostle.

The grace that Saint Ignatius invites us to pray for in Week Three is to have compassion for Jesus, suffering with him. Unlike the previous Weeks, Ignatius does not offer any of his own meditations in Week Three. It's as if the depth of Week Three is so great that it cannot be formulated into meditations. Instead, Ignatius invites us to reflect over and over on Christ's Passion and death, journeying with him through his suffering. Our imaginative prayer allows us to be with Christ in the Garden of Gethsemane, his trial, his carrying of the cross, his crucifixion, and his burial.

We are invited to enter each moment deeply, letting our hearts be united with Christ's heart. As we do, we might feel a profound meaninglessness in the things and relationships we have held dear; Christ did. We might feel abandoned by the Father and our friends and family members; Christ did. We might feel a sense of nothingness, of emptiness; Christ did. We might move through layer after layer of grief; Christ did. We don't go through such deep darkness because it's enjoyable but simply because of our love for Christ. Every other motive is burned away in the fire of love and suffering. In the language of Carmelite spirituality, it is the dark night of the soul. In the language of Ignatian spirituality, it is hard consolation.

Despite how depressing Week Three sounds, it is different from clinical depression and more profound than simply going through difficult circumstances in life. While many Christians desire the depth and intimacy of being Christ's best friend, they aren't willing to be with him in the suffering that is necessary. This often leads to men and women projecting their suffering onto Christ and considering it spiritual intimacy. They mistakenly think that the difficult circumstances in their lives are an experience of Week Three, maybe even referring to it as "hard consolation" or the "dark night of the soul." However, there are important differences between difficult circumstances like non-spiritual desolation, anxiety, or clinical depression and Week Three. The former often leave us more self-preoccupied whereas the latter will always be accompanied by the uncomfortableness of our ever-increasing transparency and vulnerability, deepening suppleness of our hearts, and the fruits of the Holy Spirit.

Those Christians who are courageous enough to enter into Week Three will often experience it as similar to accompanying a loved one through death. Monty Williams explains this experience, writing:

> Think of what happens to you when you accompany a loved one who is dying. After a while there are no words, no story, even no feeling. Emotion does not necessarily have to express itself in feeling. Instead, we experience numbness, blankness, a growing sense of meaninglessness of what might be considered socially appropriate at that time. All forms of human comfort and connection are erased. We simply wait in mystery. What remains is a radical simplicity oriented to the one Jesus calls "Abba."[8]

---

8 Williams, Monty. "Conclusion." *The Gift of Spiritual Intimacy*. Novalis Publishing Inc., 2009.

In Week Three, everything fades away and we are invited to "simply wait in mystery," which manifests itself in our willingness to meditate on the Passion narratives over and over. We allow ourselves to suffer with our best friend, Jesus, and let him suffer with us. This waiting can be so challenging that many retreatants are tempted to make a spiritual U-turn, which reveals itself in many different forms of resistance, such as falling asleep in prayer, avoiding prayer, using personal prayer time to do spiritual reading, indulging in favorite sins and false consolations, and being busy. However, for those who resist these temptations and continue to be in the mystery and intimacy of suffering with Christ, something new and beautiful begins to happen.

In the midst of the suffering, loneliness, and emptiness of being with Christ in his Passion, we begin to experience a strange consolation that I can only describe as a growing capacity to be a vessel of the Divine. In other words, rather than the emptiness being filled, it is given new meaning—it is no longer merely a void; rather, it is a vessel that is able to more fully hold and carry God and others. It is a capacity to be in the darkness of desolation without being overcome by it. This new realization doesn't happen overnight; it requires a substantial amount of prayer and surrender. Personally, I was in Week Three for over a year before I realized that the emptiness was the gift of a new capacity.

I'll never forget the moment I entered Week Three of the *Exercises*. Over the course of about two years, my spiritual director had slowly led me through the first two Weeks of the 19th Annotation retreat. In hindsight, I can see that I spent about three months resisting entering Week Three. Instead, I kept myself distracted with spiritual reading or used the meditations of Week Two during prayer. In fact, even as I prepared for an upcoming silent retreat, I assumed I would spend that week enjoying being an apostle of Jesus, companioning with him. However, the first morning of the retreat, as I was sitting down to breakfast, I was startled by the words, "Welcome to Week Three."

The words, spoken in my innermost spirit, were not said in a mean tone, but matter-of-fact, almost as if God wanted me to know that he was aware of my resistance and wanted to use the retreat to pierce through my distractions and go deeper. For the next two and a half days, I let myself enter the Scripture narratives of the Garden of Gethsemane, and I sobbed nonstop. In fact, my sobbing was so excessive that I went through a week's worth of handkerchiefs in one morning and had to start hanging them on a clothesline outside of my retreat hermitage in order to dry them out for the next prayer time. Often, as I sat in prayer, I looked out the window and saw the handkerchiefs gently blowing in the breeze like white flags signaling my surrender.

I spent about a year and a half in Week Three not because I liked it, but because I can be very resistant and obstinate. It took God that long to lovingly woo me through the process. It began with me next to Jesus in the Garden. I noticed that after weeks of praying with those Scripture accounts, I was ready to move forward, but every time I tried, God seemed to bring me back to the Garden. My spiritual director continued to encourage me to stay in the Garden where God was inviting me to be. As I did, I realized that, in the scriptural image, Jesus and I had gotten up from the ground, and the crowd was coming to arrest him. However, we couldn't move forward, because my foot was in some sort of trapdoor. I became aware that my foot was actually keeping the escape hatch open and that if I removed my foot it would close and lock.

After days of praying about what the escape hatch represented,

I realized that it was an image of some of my heart's deepest desires. Eventually, during prayer one morning, I surrendered my deepest desires and wholeheartedly chose to follow Christ. The door closed and locked as I followed Christ from the Garden to Caiaphas's house. I noticed a new freedom to move forward with Christ in his suffering.

One of the most profound and moving experiences during that time in the *Exercises* was at Jesus' trial. I was sitting beside Jesus while the Sanhedrin and guards shouted horrible things at him. At one point, he turned and looked me in the eyes, and all I saw was gratitude for my willingness to remain with him. There wasn't anger or hurt at what was being said about him, but only gratitude that he was not going through it alone. That has been a tremendous source of consolation for me ever since, especially when I've been the target of calumniation and other people's anger and hate.

Eventually, I followed Christ through his crucifixion, and I helped Joseph of Arimethea prepare his body for burial. Afterward, they put Jesus' body into a tomb, hewn from a rock. I spent my prayer time for several days just standing outside the open tomb waiting for the stone to be rolled into place. I waited and waited. Then, the Father instructed me to go into the tomb. I remember explaining to God that I didn't want to go in because someone would undoubtedly roll the stone into place and I'd be trapped! Despite my pleas, God insisted, and I eventually obeyed. Of course, as soon as I entered, the stone was moved and the tomb was sealed.

I spent hours in prayer letting myself be in Christ's tomb. At first, I remember standing against the opposite wall from Christ's body. However, as days turned into weeks, I moved closer and closer to him, eventually pulling his limp body into my lap as I sat on the stone floor with my back against the wall. I remained there, holding Christ and waiting for the resurrection. However, it wasn't time; instead, I heard the Father say to me, "Now it's your turn."

Rather than experiencing the resurrection, Jesus and I were transported back to the Garden of Gethsemane to make the whole journey again, except this time God explained that Christ was going to companion with me through *my* suffering. I did not expect that; I already felt exhausted, yet I was invited to do it all over again, but from a new perspective. It was a beautiful reminder to me that every person's journey through the *Exercises* will be distinctly different, because God's love for us is that distinct and particular.

The second time through Week Three was very different. There wasn't the consolation of Christ's gratitude for being present to him in his suffering. Instead, there was increasing darkness. The darkness became so intense at one point that I can only describe it as a felt sense that everything in the past was worthless, the future was hopeless, and the present was utterly empty. It was precisely in that emptiness that I began to experience an increasing capacity to hold God and others.

Eventually, I was buried in the tomb. This time, Jesus held my body, and we waited for the resurrection. I'll never forget the moment when it came; I had been in Week Three for about a year and a half, spending an hour to two hours every morning in prayer, and had almost become used to the darkness, emptiness, and dryness. Then, on a Saturday morning, as I sat in my prayer chair in the chapel at the rectory, my heart felt like it exploded with joy, peace, light, clarity, and love! I knew it was resurrection, and it far exceeded my expectations.

Much to my shock and surprise, God the Father, in that resurrection moment, offered me my heart's deepest desires—the very things that I had willingly sacrificed in the Garden of Gethsemane were offered back to me. I honestly could not even comprehend at the time how that would be possible or how I could be loved so deeply by God! It must have been similar to how Abraham felt when God gave Isaac back.[9] My life will never be the same, and I am filled with gratitude!

I realize that my experience of Week Three and resurrection is different from others'. As I mentioned earlier, everyone's experience of the *Exercises* is unique. Ignatius did not intend the *Exercises* to be a sort of spiritual destination but more of a spiritual roadmap that gives us a greater sense of where we are and where we're headed; but there are many different routes. Spiritual maturity always reverences the expansiveness and uniqueness of God's love and personal relationship with each person, and Ignatius shows his spiritual maturity in the expansiveness of the *Exercises*.

Those who avail themselves of the experience of Week Three receive many gifts and blessings. For example, if we've made a particular discernment and decision in Week Two, it will be tested in Week Three. If that decision is maintained and deepened through the intense purifying of Week Three, then we can be assured that it is in line with our heart's deepest desire; if not, then we re-discern. Also, we find that our faith moves beyond merely "feeling good" and enters the deeper realm of intimacy. Our false self significantly dies, as do the false constructs and paradigms we've created throughout our lives, and we enter into a love that is willing to risk death.

---

9   Genesis 22:1–19.

Week Three ends with us having journeyed with Christ in his suffering and death. We cannot choose Week Four—the Resurrection—instead, we have to patiently wait for the Father to offer it. Our entry into Week Four and how that resurrection will manifest itself are completely up to the Father. It is precisely the accumulative graces we've received so far that allow us to wait in such emptiness while anticipating new life.

Week Four

Like so much of the spiritual life, Week Four is a time when we simply let ourselves be disposed to where God is leading. Week Three required a lot of patient waiting and trusting, and so does Week Four. God, in his own time and way, will lead us into the new life he desires for us and that we most deeply desire. We generally know that God is leading us into Week Four when we find ourselves waiting in a spiritual tomb, continually opening ourselves up to the suffering of emptiness and nothingness, and when joy and clarity begin to pierce through the emptiness and nothingness.

The grace that Ignatius invites us to ask God for in Week Four is to share in the joy of Christ's resurrection. As we enter into Week Four and pray for that grace, we might find ourselves hopeful, despite our brokenness; faithful, despite the hardships; gentle and less judgmental with ourselves and others; accepting of new paradigms and ways; becoming resurrection moments for other people; empty, yet full; loving more through our actions than words; and truly joyful, not merely happy, excited, or giddy. These are, in many ways, the blessings of authentic and vulnerable love. They are the fruit of a relationship with someone who has become our beloved. And, they are very similar to the ways in which Rick grew during his long marriage to Megan.

While Rick can't pinpoint a singular moment at which he realized that Megan was his beloved, she is today. Throughout their marriage they have grown in intimacy, vulnerability, and mutuality. In particular, their mutuality—their willingness to share everything they have and everything they are—has helped shape Rick's character. For example, Rick explained how he was a bit of a "hothead" when he was a young man. He easily became angry and often retaliated when he felt slighted. Megan's gentleness seems to have worn off on him. He is more accepting of other people, including their faults.

Whereas he used to anchor his identity in what he did for a living, his political affiliation, and what clubs and organizations he belonged to, Rick now senses that his identity is rooted in his love for God, Megan, and his family. His mutual love with Megan has brought him a peace and steadfastness unlike anything he could have imagined—a peace and steadfastness that has allowed him and his wife to weather many storms throughout their marriage. These are the very graces we experience in Week Four.

Ignatius invites us to experience the blessings of Week Four by first meditating on Mary, the mother of Jesus, encountering him after his resurrection. While such a scene is not explicit in sacred Scripture, Ignatius believed that it was implicit in the mention that the risen Christ had appeared to many others (1 Corinthians 15:6). In this meditation, Ignatius invites us to be with Mary as we reflect on what it means to have our emptiness, grief, anger, hopelessness, and fear be transformed into joy, peace, hope, and trust. He then invites retreatants to meditate on other resurrection and ascension accounts in the gospels, such as the risen Christ's encounters with Mary Magdalene, Thomas, and the disciples on the road to Emmaus.

As we continue spending time meditating on the resurrection and ascension narratives in Week Four, we humbly realize that we are present at the moment when the Father answered Jesus' deepest desire. It's hard to fathom such an amazing reality. The closest analogy I can come up with is being suddenly present when a young man drops to one knee in front of his girlfriend and proposes marriage. As bystanders, we undoubtedly feel privileged, humbled, hopeful, and almost embarrassed to be part of something so scandalously intimate!

This is what we might feel when we realize that we are spiritually present at a moment of great intimacy between Christ and the Father. Jesus expressed many times throughout the gospels his deepest desire—to be beside the Father—and he received that gift![10] Monty Williams explains what that gift does in our hearts, writing:

> Resurrection allows us to admit our deepest desire in all of its raw urgency, because we see in the Father's raising Christ from the dead that [his] desire is answered. We experience the joy of the resurrection when we let ourselves admit that our deepest desire can and will be answered.[11]

Of course, he is referring to deep desires, not superficial ones. Throughout our journey in the Exercises, our superficial desires have been greatly purged and we desire deep and eternal gifts. Those deep desires lead us to the apex of the *Exercises*, the "Contemplation to Attain Divine Love," found at the end of Week Four.

---

10 A few examples include: John 14:28; Matthew 26:64; John 13:3.

11 Williams, Monty. "The Ascension." *The Gift of Spiritual Intimacy*.

The Contemplation to Attain Divine Love

Throughout the spiritual direction training program, we read a lot of books about the *Spiritual Exercises*. I found that all of them ended with just a brief mention of the "Contemplation to Attain Divine Love." None of them unpacked the spiritual blessings and implications of that important section of the *Exercises*. This contemplation is too important for us to just gloss over and, therefore, the rest of this book can be understood as an invitation for us to look deeply at the blessings, implications, and spiritual practices that are inherent in the scandalous intimacy of the "Contemplation to Attain Divine Love."

Despite its title, the "Contemplation to Attain Divine Love" is not an invitation to try to obtain God's love, since we have already received it. Instead, the title is meant to be an invitation to contemplate how we can love as God loves and experience deeper intimacy with him. It begins with Saint Ignatius reminding us of two important truths—love is demonstrated more by actions than by words, and love is ultimately defined by mutuality. While these might seem a bit obvious to most of us, Ignatius clearly thought they were worth mentioning. And our own experience reminds us that the most obvious things in life are often the things we most quickly forget.

Ignatius wrote, "Love ought to manifest itself in deeds rather than in words."[12] This isn't just a description about how God loves us; it also describes how God desires us to love him. I learned this several years ago when I read Dr. Gary Chapman's bestselling book *The Five Love Languages*. In the book Dr. Chapman

---

12　Puhl, Louis J. *The Spiritual Exercises of St. Ignatius: Based on Studies in the Language of the Autograph*. Loyola Press, 1968.

reminds us that love can be expressed in many different ways, including through "words of affirmation, quality time, receiving gifts, acts of service, [and] physical touch."[13] As I read, I learned more about my primary love language and also took the information into personal prayer, reflecting on *God's* primary love language.

Wondering what the Bible said about how God desires to be loved, I found that sacred Scripture is filled with examples of God accepting all five expressions, or languages, of love. However, I noticed that the gospel accounts of Christ's life seem to suggest that his primary love language is "acts of service." In other words, God likes for us to put our love into action!

We don't find many New Testament stories indicating that Jesus desired human touch, words of affirmation, or gifts. There are several Scripture passages, however, that would lead us to believe that Jesus did appreciate the gift of quality time with others, in particular, close friends like Martha, Mary, Lazarus, Peter, James, and John. Based on the gospels, though, one could argue that Christ preferred acts of service even more than quality time with friends. It was undoubtedly important to Jesus for faith and love to be put into action. For example, in the Gospel of Matthew, Jesus explained that "acts of service" is the love language that distinguishes the sheep from the goats.

> The king will say to those on his right, "Come, you who are blessed by my Father. Inherit the kingdom prepared for you from the foundation of the world. For I was hungry and you

---

13 Chapman, Gary. *The Five Love Languages: The Secret to Love that Lasts.* Northfield Publishing, p. 122.

gave me food, I was thirsty and you gave me drink, a stranger
and you welcomed me, naked and you clothed me, ill and you
cared for me, in prison and you visited me." Then the righteous
will answer him and say, "Lord, when did we see you hungry
and feed you, or thirsty and give you drink? When did we see
you a stranger and welcome you, or naked and clothe you?
When did we see you ill or in prison, and visit you?" And the
king will say to them in reply, "Amen, I say to you, whatever
you did for one of these least brothers of mine, you did for me."

MATTHEW 25:34–40

Another scriptural example of Christ's desire for love to be
expressed in deed more than in words is in chapter seven of the
Gospel of Matthew. Jesus said, "Not everyone who says to me,
'Lord, Lord,' will enter the kingdom of heaven, but only the one
who *does the will* of my Father in heaven" (Matthew 7:21 [*emphasis mine*]). Love, then, must be put into action. We experience
God's love in a powerful way when he puts it into action, and he
experiences our love in a beautiful way when we do the same.

Saint Ignatius not only understood this important truth about
love, he also understood that love is defined by mutuality, and
mutuality is defined as the quality or state of sharing between two
or more people or groups. According to Ignatius, this includes a
sharing of goods and a sharing of selves.[14]

By and large, we are comfortable with the idea of God sharing his "goods" with us, such as the food we eat, water we drink,
virtues we possess, jobs we work, knowledge we obtain, and possessions we own. It's relatively easy to be grateful for the role the

---

14 *Spiritual Exercises*, #231, #234.

Creator of the universe played in the gifts we possess. However, we tend to be less comfortable with the idea that mutual love involves God sharing his very *Self* with us—an invitation into the communal life of the Trinity! In his book *Finding God in All Things*, William A. Barry expresses this invitation beautifully as he writes, "God shares with us not just physical life on this planet, a gift enough, but wants to share with us God's own community life. God is continually creating this universe with the one intention of inviting all persons into the communal life of the Trinity."[15]

The idea of God sharing his very Self causes most of us to emotionally default to a deep sense of unworthiness as well as fear of becoming presumptuous in our relationship with him. Yet the gospels clearly show us that God desires mutuality with us. For example, Jesus told the Apostles, "I no longer call you slaves, because a slave does not know what his master is doing. I have called you friends, because I have told you everything I have heard from my Father" (John 15:15). To be a friend of God— living in mutual love with him—means that we let ourselves be completely vulnerable, sharing our hopes and dreams, loves and desires, strengths and gifts, weaknesses and fears, resentments and hates, defensiveness and idiosyncrasies, favorite sins and addictions, and...well, everything. Wow! Imagine what happens in our hearts and in our lives when we so radically and intimately share ourselves with God!

Jesus took our intimacy with God even beyond friendship, expressing his desire to share with the Apostles (and now us) the very life of the Trinity, praying to the Father, "I have given them the glory you gave me, so that they may be one, as we are one, I in them and you in me, and that they may be brought to perfection as one...I made known to them your name and I will make it known, that the love with which you loved me may be in them and I in them" (John 17:22–23a, 26). We are invited to be wholly consumed by God's life, yet not annihilated, and to wholeheartedly consume God, yet not turn him into merely a projection of our egos. In a way that is similar to marriage: two become one in our mutuality with God.

For those who make the long journey through the *Exercises* and arrive at this contemplation on mutual love, there is a clear sense that our relationship with God entails reverence more than unworthiness. When most of us began our spiritual journey with God, unworthiness was the primary point of reference in our relationship with him. As we grew in intimacy with God, however, we accepted the radical truth that the God of the universe desires mutuality with us, and such intimacy is possible without falling into the sin of presumption. We also accepted that God doesn't just reserve this special friendship for canonized saints and otherworldly mystics; it's a mutuality open to all of us. William A. Barry explains this, writing:

> Ignatius presupposes that God wants complete mutuality with us. He is talking about the Creator of the universe here, the God who needs nothing, who creates out of love, not necessity. Ignatius has discovered in his own experience that God wants mutuality, wants the love of friendship to obtain between God and himself and, therefore, between God and every human being. He found this discovery reinforced by his reading of Scripture and by his experience of directing others. Thus, God

wants to be our dearest friend, our tremendous lover, and our beloved.[16]

In Saint Ignatius' understanding, to embrace mutuality with God also requires us to embrace a profound mutuality with all of creation—everything and everyone. In this way, "our love becomes more universal and embraces all that God dreams for our world."[17] This new revelation might very well cause more resistance in us than the idea of mutuality with God! We are invited to face our fear of being lovingly vulnerable and transparent with everything and everyone. With courage, we are challenged to reach out to others, sharing our goods and our very selves. Martin Luther King Jr. understood the depth of this mutuality when he wrote in his famous "Letter from Birmingham Jail":

> All life is interrelated. We are caught in an inescapable network of mutuality; tied in a single garment of destiny. Whatever affects one directly, affects all indirectly. As long as there is poverty in this world, no man can be totally rich even if he has a billion dollars. As long as diseases are rampant and millions of people cannot expect to live more than twenty or thirty years, no man can be totally healthy, even if he just got a clean bill of health from the finest clinic in America. Strangely enough, I can never be what I ought to be until you are what you ought to be. You can never be what you ought to be until I am what I ought to be.

---

16 Barry, William A. *Letting God Come Close*. Loyola Press, 2001, pp. 182-83.

17 Barry. *Letting God Come Close*. p. 184.

Such mutuality and interconnectedness with all of creation cause us to grow in a radical gentleness and acceptance because we realize that harshness and unkindness toward God's creation harmfully affect everything. We are only as loving as we are to the "least" of creation. I became aware of this important gentleness and acceptance during the months that I reflected on the "Contemplation to Attain Divine Love." For example, there was a fruit fly buzzing around my office, yet I didn't feel the need to kill it or get rid of it. I simply let it be present, as I, too, was present.

I remember the fruit fly being there for several days when an engaged couple came into my office for marriage preparation. As we were talking, the husband-to-be said, "There's a gnat in here." Just as I began to explain the sacred place the gnat had in my office and the role it played on my spiritual journey, the man's hands clapped together with ninja-like precision, sending the gnat to its glory. Gentleness isn't easy. Acceptance isn't easy. Mutuality isn't easy. And, if we're brutally honest, we'll admit that gentleness, acceptance, and mutuality are often more easily expressed toward a fruit fly than toward the annoying person we try to avoid at church each Sunday.

Through the "Contemplation to Attain Divine Love," as well as the other meditations in Week Four, we experience that our very lives have become living gospels, our brokenness has new meaning, there are no limits to God's love or our love, life is filled with wonder and creativity, God is a mystery (and so are we and others), all of creation is interconnected, and we see in new ways. Both during prayer and outside of personal prayer time, our mutuality with God draws us into the truth that love is generous and vulnerable despite the stinginess and self-preservation surrounding us in the world. Love is union with the beloved despite the exclusion promoted by the world. Love is work despite the message of self-entitlement we hear every day. And love is completely unmerited despite the fact that we live in a world often defined by merit. We have fallen in love, been rescued in our woundedness, companioned with Christ, suffered with him, and accepted that we are his beloved and live in mutual love with him!

REFLECTION QUESTIONS

1. What Week of the *Exercises* do you feel best describes your relationship with God right now? Why?

2. How does Rick and Megan's relationship help you better understand your relationship with God?

3. Who is the one person in your life to whom you have made yourself the most vulnerable and transparent? What characteristics about that person helped you to be vulnerable and transparent to him or her?

4. Who is the one person in your life with whom you have the hardest time being vulnerable and transparent? Why?

5. What are the most important gifts that God has shared with you?

6. How have you experienced God sharing his very Self with you?

7. What gifts do you regularly share with God? How does God thank you?

8. Recall a time when you shared your very self with God. What did it look like? What did it feel like?

9. Most people are initially resistant to the idea of mutuality with God. What are your hesitations?

CHAPTER THREE

Discerning the Relationship

We make judgments about relationships every day. This might happen subtly as we plan our weekends and decide whom we want to hang around with and whom we want to avoid, or it might be more explicit, like labeling someone on our social media a "close friend" or an "acquaintance." Knowing the depth of various relationships in our lives helps us to know what, if any, next step we need to take for greater intimacy. The same is true in our relationship with God. Saint Ignatius of Loyola gave us a roadmap of our relationship with God in his *Spiritual Exercises*, which can help us to know where we are and where we are heading.

Ultimately, the goal of our relationship with God is the intimacy of mutual friendship.

While Ignatius defined mutuality and encouraged it, the *Exercises* do not go into much detail about the practicalities of that intimacy. In this chapter, I will pick up where Ignatius left off. I'll unpack the implications and practicalities of mutual intimacy with God by defining personal prayer and suggesting some marks, or indicators, that can help us discern the depth of our relationship with God. In doing so, we begin to see how mutual intimacy with God is similar to mutual intimacy with others.

What Is Personal Prayer?

I define personal prayer as single-minded relational time with God that cultivates a deeper, more authentic love and awareness of God, ourselves, others, and creation. As such, personal prayer is different from communal prayer—when we pray *with* others— and intercessory prayer—when we pray *for* others. Instead, personal prayer is special one-on-one time with God. This definition of personal prayer is not meant to be restrictive, nor is it meant to be a benchmark that feeds our egos and makes us feel like we've "accomplished" the task of spiritual growth. Instead, it is meant to encourage greater intimacy with God. In order to better understand personal prayer, let's look at some of the key words and phrases in my definition.

When I say that personal prayer is *single-minded*, I mean that it ideally avoids multitasking. Most of us are really good at multitasking, including during prayer. We pray while we do the laundry. We pray while we drive. While multitasking is fine for intercessory prayer, personal prayer ideally entails setting everything else aside so that we can be fully present to God. By doing so, we reverence the importance of what we have to say to God and the importance of what God has to say to us. We find something similar in our human relationships.

When a husband is enjoying a football game on TV and his wife asks him about the weather, he will more than likely continue watching the game while he talks to her because the topic of conversation is fairly mundane. But, if she sits down next to him and says, "Honey, we're pregnant!" he will turn off the TV, turn toward her, and give her his full attention (we hope). If we tend to think of our personal prayer as time spent with God talking about mundane and trivial things, we will probably multitask while praying. However, if we reverence that there are really important things that we want to share with God and God wants to share with us, we will set everything else aside and be single-minded during prayer.

Personal prayer is also *relational time* spent with God. In other words, it is time spent sharing the deepest, most important movements of our hearts. This is not easy! We often fear such vulnerability and transparency. Sometimes it's easier and feels safer to simply let our personal prayer become time for Scripture study or spiritual reading. At other times, it's more comfortable to fill up our personal prayer time telling God what he needs to do, whom he needs to bless, how he needs to forgive, and where he needs to manifest himself. We might avoid taking time to listen to God in prayer, finding it easier to believe that he isn't interested in speaking to us. We might find it safer to believe that God is "out there" and we are "down here." It might feel less overwhelming to think about God's care for us as being more like how the president of the United States cares for Americans than like how a lover cares for his beloved. Regardless of the creative ways we avoid sharing with God the most important movements of our hearts, they keep our personal prayer from being relational.

In addition to personal prayer being single-minded and relational, it is also time spent *with God*. While that might seem obvious, it's amazing how easy it is to turn prayer into a conversation with ourselves rather than a dialogue with God. Years ago, I heard a man say that many Catholics go to Eucharistic Adoration and spend an hour adoring themselves. This gentleman was expressing how easy it is for us to finish our prayer time without having consciously spent time with God. Personal prayer can easily become just "one more thing" to check off our to-do list, and when it does, we often spend our prayer preoccupied with what we need to get accomplished rather than focusing on God.

Lastly, personal prayer should *cultivate* a deeper, more authentic love and awareness of God, ourselves, others, and creation. This is just a fancy way of saying that our prayer should bear fruit. If we have been praying a particular way for years and we find ourselves growing angrier, more hateful, impatient, unkind, abrasive, and controlling, then we need to find a new way to pray! It might be that we are spending a considerable amount of time in prayer each day, but it's not relational prayer; it's not connecting our heart in intimacy with the heart of Christ.

While there's no one right way to pray, personal prayer is rightly defined and judged by the fruit it bears in our relationships with God, ourselves, others, and creation. When our hearts deeply connect with God in prayer we find the fruits of the Spirit listed by Paul in his letter to the Galatians being manifested, namely, "love, joy, peace, patience, kindness, generosity, faithfulness, gentleness, [and] self-control" (Galatians 5:22–23). In addition to these fruits, we might also find ourselves growing in the

Beatitudes,[18] the theological virtues[19] and the corporal and spiritual works of mercy.[20]

Take a moment to consider a time when your personal prayer consisted of these four important aspects—*single-minded, relational time with God that cultivates spiritual fruit*. What was the experience like and when did it happen? For Beatrice, it happened just five weeks before she died. When she came to my office for spiritual direction the first time, she was filled with anger. It was clear that she had desired an intimate relationship with God her entire life yet feared what that intimacy required.

She began our meeting focused on her distaste with the Song of Songs in the Old Testament, also known as the Song of Solomon. She explained that it was "too intimate" and "should not be in the Bible." At the end of our session, I encouraged her to read the Song of Songs as the author intended—as a play—with her taking the part of the bride and God taking the part of the groom. At the age of 82, she was fearful, but willing.

Beatrice returned to my office a couple of weeks later filled with joy. She explained how she finally understood the Song of Songs, and more importantly, she finally understood that God was madly in love with her! She had experienced relational prayer! That particular Scripture allowed her to finally express her deep love for God without feeling embarrassed or shameful, and it allowed her to fearlessly hear God's unconditional love for her. This became a particularly important consolation for both Beatrice and her family when she died about a month later.

---

18 Matthew 5:3–11; Luke 6:20–22.

19 1 Corinthians 13:13.

20 Matthew 25:34–40.

Beatrice's experience reminds us that God is clearly not sat-
isfied with simply creating us or even saving us. He has continually revealed through Scripture, creation, and Jesus Christ that
he desires to be in an intimate, unique, and personal relationship
with us. Our personal prayer is an essential component to that
intimate relationship with God, just as meaningful conversations
are essential to lovers. Let's look, then, at some of the marks of an
intimate relationship with God that has been deepened through
relational prayer.

Marks of Relationality with God
Knowing some of the marks of healthy human relationships can
help us to discern our relationship with God and the relationality of our prayer. For example, most of us have experienced the
important differences between casual and intimate human relationships. Casual relationships are driven by our own needs,
while intimate relationships are driven by the other person's
needs. Another way of saying this is that immature love looks
after its own needs while mature, authentic love selflessly desires
what is best for the other.

When we are in a casual relationship with God, it is often all
about us. We want God to do this or that. We need him to fix this
or that. We go to church and pray primarily because we don't want
to feel guilty or because we hope it will help us get what we want.

A deeper, more mature relationship with God primarily focuses
on God. We find ourselves wondering what we can do to please
God because we love him. We desire to be in church because of
what we can bring to God through our praise and gratitude, as well
as what we can bring to others through our loving presence. Such
selflessness is a mark of our healthy and relational love for God.

In addition to intimacy being deepened by selflessness, there are numerous other marks of healthy human relationships that we can apply to our relationship with God. Psychology helps us name such marks. Many psychologists agree that the following characteristics are the most common marks of healthy human friendships:

Honesty • Communication • Shared responsibility
Respect • Trust • Support • Commitment
Specialness • Sense of playfulness/fondness

Using these characteristics, as well as others, I have formulated the following eleven marks of a healthy relationship with God. When our personal prayer remains deeply relational, we will more than likely see these marks evident in our friendship with God; they will help us to be confident that we have a personal, intimate relationship with him. I have included some questions for each mark and hope they are helpful in discerning the ways in which your friendship with God can grow in intimacy and mutuality.

1. Friends are grateful for one another.

Healthy relationships are saturated in gratitude. Without regular expressions of appreciation, friends and lovers will eventually feel used and unappreciated. The same thing is true in our relationship with God. This is undoubtedly why sacred Scripture is filled with reminders for us to thank God. For example, Saint Paul instructs us to "persevere in prayer, being watchful in it with thanksgiving" (Colossians 4:2). Also, the New Testament word "eucharist" means "thanksgiving" and was an essential quality of the early Christian community.

Not only is it important for us to express our appreciation for God and what he does for us, it's also important for us to receive God's appreciation. Healthy relationships require such reciprocity.

- When was the last time you let God thank you for who you are and what you do for him?

This might include receiving his gratitude through the words and actions of others, or simply through his Holy Spirit speaking to you during personal prayer. Any resistance within us to letting God thank us is a reminder that we still have room to grow in our mutuality with God.

2. Friends admire each other.

What do you admire most about your best friend? Maybe it's her deep kindness and acceptance of others, or her generosity. Most of us are conscious of the gifts we most admire in our friends, and more than likely, they have shared what they most admire about us. This is a mark of a healthy friendship. The same is true in our relationship with God.

When our prayer is relational, we find ourselves aware of what we most admire about Christ and are open to hearing him share with us what he most admires about us. We primarily learn what we most admire about Christ through our knowledge of him in the gospels, and we primarily come to know what he most admires about us through others and through prayer.

- What do you admire most about Christ right now in your spiritual journey? What does Christ admire most about you?

3. Friends desire to become more like one another.

Often, the very things we admire in our friends are the things we desire to emulate. Take for example Ruth and Naomi. In the biblical book named after her, Ruth expressed her desire to become more like Naomi, saying, "Wherever you go I will go, wherever you lodge I will lodge. Your people shall be my people and your God, my God" (Ruth 1:16). Just as she desired to become more like her friend, we find a similar thing in our relationship with God.

Recently in prayer, I reflected on the core values that guide my life and ministry and compared them to Jesus' core values. These meditations have been very fruitful and beautiful, especially as I continue to discover values in Jesus that I desire to imitate. It has opened up new dialogues with Christ and new experiences of intimacy with him.

- What aspect of Christ's personality and service do you most deeply desire to imitate?

Through personal prayer, our response to this question will move beyond such generalities as "everything," as we find ourselves answering in very specific ways, such as, "to serve the least among us," or "to bless the person who has hurt me the most" or "to accept the blessing of poverty." Such answers indicate that we have truly come to know Christ and we desire to mirror his gifts.

4. Friends feel a sense of oneness with one another.

The union that exists between intimate friends is often manifested physically, mentally, emotionally, and spiritually. For example, really close friends often feel comfortable in one another's personal space, which might include hugging, kissing, holding hands, or wrapping their arms around one another. These are things that we may not feel comfortable doing with a stranger.

Also, intimate friends are often mentally on the same proverbial page—they complete one another's sentences, hold many of the same ideologies, and share a similar education. They might even experience an emotional oneness by intuitively knowing when the other person is hurting, angry, or sad. Their spiritual oneness might be manifested in shared prayers, intercession, and common faith. All of the manifestations of oneness that we find in intimate human friendships are available in our intimacy with God.

Jesus indicated the level of oneness he desires with each of us when he prayed to the Father, "I have given them the glory you gave me, so that they may be one, as we are one, I in them and you in me, that they may be brought to perfection as one" (John 17:22–23). Our oneness with Christ, modeled on his oneness with the Father, might manifest itself in shared ways of thinking, knowing what the other is feeling, or spending time praying with one another.

- When have you felt the closest to God? Was that oneness manifested physically, mentally, emotionally, or spiritually? What did it teach you about God's love for you?

5. Friends have fun together.

While there are undoubtedly some very serious moments in friendship, there should also be lighthearted, laughter-infused, and joyful moments. This is not only true in our human relationships, but also in our relationship with God. An indicator of the healthiness of our relationship with God is that we have fun with him, laugh together, and even share inside jokes.

I remember years ago, while on a silent retreat, God referred to me as his "little hobo." Various interesting and quirky things happened in the days that followed that helped me to better understand what that term of endearment meant to God, and it also brought both of us a lot of joy and giggles.

This particular mark of a healthy relationship is very important in our friendship with God, because, if we don't occasionally experience such levity, then our image of God might be too restrictive. We might still be relating to God as if he is primarily a fixer or judge, which I'll say more about in the next chapter. When our relationship with God is one of mutual friendship, which doesn't negate reverence, it allows room for fun and humor.

- When do you and God have the most fun together? When do you both laugh the hardest? When was the last time you and God planned a fun event together, such as a date night?

6. Friends think about one another often.

They think about one another even when they are not physically together. A similar thing can be said about our friendship with God. Many of my directees have shared with me their desire to remember God more throughout the day. They don't want to limit their friendship with God or their thoughts about him to just the time they spend in personal prayer.

Their desire often leads to the fruit of thinking about God more throughout the day. They experience an increased continuity between the time they spend in prayer and the rest of their day. For example, if during their personal prayer time in the morning they talked to God about their desire to be more merciful, they might find themselves talking to God throughout the day about situations that require mercy.

As a way of responding to this desire, I recommend that people use their cell phones to remind them to think about God more throughout the day and continue the conversation they started with him during personal prayer. For example, they might change the wallpaper on their phone to an image or a word that reminds them of the grace they are praying for or use the alarm on their phone for periodic reminders to include God in their day. Notes stuck in important places like the steering wheel or the bathroom mirror can also be helpful in forming a greater habit of thinking of God throughout the day. Regardless of how high-tech or low-tech our methods, they are reflections of our desire to think about God more frequently throughout the day.

- What has been the most important topic of conversation you've had with God recently in prayer? In what way do you desire to continue that conversation with God throughout each day? Are there any specific times throughout the day that you would like to think more about God?

7. *Friends communicate everything with one another.*

Healthy relationships are built on such deep trust and respect that there are no taboo topics. In other words, friends can talk about anything and everything while always keeping the conversations respectful and gentle. The same is true in our relationship with God. The healthiest friendships with God entail such a beautiful openness that anything can be expressed in prayer, even our anger at him and our struggles with sin.

I've had numerous directees tell me that they don't feel comfortable sharing certain things with God, such as anger or sinfulness. They fear God's reaction. Their reluctance to share these things helps them to see the ways in which their friendship with God needs to grow in relationality. I've had other directees who argued with me about the importance of sharing everything with God, reminding me that he already knows everything so there should be no need to talk to him about everything, especially uncomfortable or intimate things. The truth, however, is that until we share what is important to us, we have not entered into intimacy with God. A husband might know his wife loves him, but they have not entered an essential place of intimacy and vulnerability in their relationship until she says, "I love you."

- What is the single most uncomfortable topic you can think of discussing with God? Why? What grace would you need from God in order to share your deepest feelings about that topic?

8. Friends reminisce.

They take time to remember the good times and to savor the ways in which they have grown together. Saint Ignatius recommends that you and I take time to spiritually reminisce with God, savoring the best moments. Ignatius called this practice "repetition" and described it as taking time to remember a previous experience of consolation in order to further savor it. For example, Meredith began coming to spiritual direction after a deeply moving experience of God's love for her.

While on a pilgrimage in Italy, she heard God speak to her for the very first time. In the silence of an Italian Gothic cathedral in Orvieto, Meredith was startled by the words, "I have not abandoned you." The words were not audible; they were more profound than sound. She knew in her core that God was with her. Such an experience of consolation should not be quickly skimmed over. During our spiritual direction sessions, Meredith savored God's words by describing the nuances of how they made her feel. In her personal prayer time she reminisced about the experience, reflecting on several Scripture verses that echo the same sentiments God shared with her in Orvieto.

- When was the last time you reminisced with a close friend? What would you want to reminisce about with God? What was the last consolation you experienced from God? How was he present before, during, and after the experience? How did you grow from the experience?

9. Friends trust one another.

Since love requires vulnerability, trust is essential to healthy relationships. If we don't trust that our friends cherish and respect our character, personality, opinion, body, faith, and values, then we will never fully give ourselves to them. This is also true in our relationship with God.

In order for us to have a healthy friendship with God, we must trust him, and he must trust us. Our trust in God must move beyond an infantile hope that God will fix things or give us what we want. Instead, our trust is that he is always with us and always for us; we trust that he cherishes and respects us.

It is also important that we have a sense of God's trust in us. His trust is often manifested in his willingness to let us participate in the life of his beloved sons and daughters. For example, when God burdens our hearts with someone—inviting us to intercede for him or her—he is entrusting us with that person. He is trusting that we will not share with others what he showed us about that person's need for prayer.

God shows his trust in other ways as well, such as letting us care for others, inviting us to be a part of a particular church, choosing us to do a certain ministry, letting us make a meal for someone, inviting us to tithe, or asking us to listen to someone. It's no small thing that we trust God and that he trusts us. It is an essential part of our healthy relationship with him.

- In what ways have you experienced trusting God, and him trusting you? Has God ever entrusted you with something or someone that caused you fear or anxiety?

10. Friends can name one another's favorite things.
If a friendship is relatively new or not much deeper than an acquaintanceship, then we might only know a person's favorite

color, hobby, or food. However, as the friendship deepens, we learn more important things like his or her favorite Scripture verse, childhood memory, value, or book. The same thing is true in our relationship with God—the deeper it is, the more we will know about his favorite things.

As I've previously mentioned, throughout the years, I have enjoyed spending time in personal prayer meditating on some of God's favorite things, like his favorite love language and his favorite values. The Bible offers us a wealth of information about God's other favorite things, such as his favorite form of prayer, type of person, quality of character, act of mercy, and manifestation of love. Learning God's favorite things during personal prayer and comparing them to our favorite things is an intimate and beautiful experience.

- Have you ever spent your prayer time learning about God's favorite things? What would you want to learn about first?

11. Friends have a special love language.
This often happens without them consciously intending to create it. For example, lovers might end their texts with a special emoji, or they might express special forms of affection for greetings and departures. Such unique and personal signs of love can also be found in our intimate relationship with God.

In the book of Genesis, God offered Noah a special sign of his love—the rainbow. God told him, "This is the sign of the covenant that I am making between me and you and every living creature with you for all ages to come: I set my bow in the clouds to serve as a sign of the covenant between me and the earth"

(Genesis 9:12–13). While our own expressions of love with God might not be quite that dramatic, they are no less special.

Years ago, one of my directees shared with me that when he was a child, his father frequently got drunk and beat him. He explained that after one of the first beatings, he went to his room and looked out the window, crying and feeling very alone. Then, a huge butterfly landed on the windowpane. As it gently flapped its wings, he felt God's presence and love. He also knew that God loved his father and desired to heal him. From that moment to the present, every time the man sees a butterfly, he is reminded that God loves him and is with him. Butterflies have become a special language of love between them.

- What are the special ways that God reveals his love for you? What are the special things that you do to communicate your love to God?

I hope that my definition of personal prayer and the eleven marks of healthy friendships encourage you to continue to deepen your intimacy with God through personal prayer. As you might imagine, deepening one's intimacy with God will require us to change and move beyond the impediments of mutuality. In the next chapter, I point out some obstacles that hinder our deepening intimacy with God. Before you start reading that chapter, however, I encourage you to spend some time with the following reflection questions, meditating on the blessings and struggles you are currently experiencing in your personal prayer.

REFLECTION QUESTIONS

1. How much time would you ideally like to spend in personal prayer each day?

2. What one thing most frequently keeps you from regularly praying?

3. What is the current structure for your personal prayer time? In other words, how do you spend your time in prayer?

4. In what way does God usually communicate to you?

5. Draw a pie chart that shows how much of your personal prayer time is spent sharing your heart with God, how much is spent listening to God, and how much is spent doing other things (reading, interceding for others, ruminating about the past, worrying about the future, etc.).

6. Similar to the previous exercise, draw a pie chart that shows what your prayer time would *ideally* look like.

CHAPTER FOUR

Obstacles to Intimacy

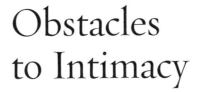

As children, many of us were told, "Nothing worthwhile comes easy." This parental mantra was clearly mom and dad's way of getting us to do something difficult and to do it without complaining. They were loosely quoting Theodore Roosevelt who said, "Nothing in the world is worth having or worth doing unless it means effort, pain, [and] difficulty." While we may have rolled our eyes years ago at this message, most of us have come to understand its truth, especially regarding the challenges of love.

The intimacy and mutuality of love that we desire will necessarily entail effort, pain, and difficulty. It will require us to be

honest about the numerous obstacles to love in our lives, such as
our skewed image of God and ourselves, sin, anger, ego, unforgiveness, fear, and clutter. Let's take a brief look at each of these
and how they hinder the intimacy we desire to have with God.

Our Image of God

Psychology has helped us to see more clearly the effects of our
unhealthy images of others. When a relationship with a beloved
is mostly a projection of what we are unable to love within ourselves, the relationship is marked with dependency, codepen-
dency, fear, irrational expectations, neediness, insecurities,
disappointments, and anger. Such dysfunctional relationships
do not have the capacity to hold the gift of mutuality. Instead,
mutual love requires a healthy image and understanding of the
beloved. This is just as true in our relationship with God as it is in
our human relationships.

Unfortunately, we live in a world filled with many skewed
images of God and misunderstandings about him. God is often
not much more than a projection of our egos. We frequently put
him in the proverbial box, demanding that he be what we want.
Such an approach to our relationship with God hinders the gift
of mutuality, which will always challenge us to let God define
himself. However, this can be really hard; it is difficult for us to
let go of our unhealthy images of God because we've had them for
so long and they help us to feel in control of life.

I remember being told years ago, "If you still have the same
image of God today that you had as a child, something is wrong."
I was convicted that day! I realized that my image of God was *precisely* the same as it was during my childhood. While it was not a
blatantly unhealthy image, it seemed increasingly restrictive. Yet

I had held onto it for most of my life because it was comfortable and familiar. I'm not the only one. Many of my directees struggle in prayer for many years before they find the courage and capacity to let God be more than their restrictive images.

In my opinion, the two most popular unhealthy images of God in the world today include God as the fixer and as the judge. While we can legitimately say that God possesses nuances of both of these roles, they are not his essence. When we move from naming a part of something to claiming that part as the entirety of something, we usually limit ourselves. In fact, a professor in seminary told us that a heresy is just a truth taken to an extreme; we might say something similar about our unhealthy images of God. They are often *aspects* of God's essence taken to be his *entire* essence. This is the case with the image of God as the fixer.

We find many popular theologies today that promote the image of God as fixer, such as the "prosperity gospel." Often, these theologies teach that if we have enough faith or if we pray properly, God will fix what we need him to fix and do what we need him to do. Several years ago I was reminded of just how unhealthy this image is when I visited a woman whose husband was battling cancer. He and another cancer patient, a pentecostal man, had been roommates at the hospital. After the pentecostal man died, the woman went to his visitation and was shocked when she heard members of the man's church saying things to the widow like, "If you had only had more faith, God would have healed your husband" and "He wouldn't have died if he had believed in God's healing power." I can't imagine how traumatic that must have been for the faith-filled and prayerful widow as she grieved the death of her husband. That story is a good, albeit extreme, example of the skewed image of God as the fixer.

Undoubtedly, members of the widow's church would defend their image of God by pointing out various New Testament verses that seem to present a theology of God as the fixer. For example, in the Gospel of Matthew, Jesus says, "If you have faith the size of a mustard seed, you will say to this mountain, 'Move from here to there,' and it will move. Nothing will be impossible for you" (Matthew 17:20). On the surface, this seems to indicate that God desires to do what we ask him to do and that his action is dependent on the depth of our faith. However, we know Scripture always invites us to read with expanded hearts, never taking verses out of context or superficially reading them.

In context, this passage follows the story of the Transfiguration of Christ, where he is presented as the new Moses. And, just as Moses came down from the mountaintop and found that the Israelites had lost their faith in Yahweh, Jesus came down the mountain and found a lack of faith. This story, then, has less to do with our prayer or faith controlling God's power and more to do with Christ being the new Moses who is leading us toward a new relationship with God.

Other New Testament stories that have kept many people holding onto the image of God as the fixer are the various miracles that Christ performed. Christ is the full revelation of the Father,[21] so if Christ fixed illnesses and demonic possessions, then one could quickly conclude that God must primarily be interested in such things. However, as we read the miracle accounts in the gospels, we find that there are several reasons for Jesus' healings and exorcisms that have little to do with fixing people's problems.

---

21 John 14:8–9.

First, we know that Jesus healed simply out of love for people. In the Gospel of Matthew, chapter nine, we read, "When [Jesus] saw the crowds, he had compassion on them, because they were harassed and helpless, like sheep without a shepherd" (9:36, NIV). Rather than minimizing Christ's compassion to a superficial desire to fix our problems, we are invited to see in it Christ's love and care for us; he sees our pain.

Christ's compassion and love are even more profound than just healing someone who needed healing; they allowed the ill to be part of the faith community again. To be sick or possessed in ancient Judaism meant to be separated from the community of believers, to be an outcast. It was assumed that if a person was sick or possessed, he or she must have committed some serious sins and, therefore, they were kept away from the Temple. Healings and exorcisms were gateways back into the faith community like in the story of the leper from the Gospel of Matthew:

> When Jesus came down from the mountain, great crowds followed him. And then a leper approached, did him homage, and said, "Lord, if you wish, you can make me clean." He stretched out his hand, touched him, and said, "I will do it. Be made clean." His leprosy was cleansed immediately. Then Jesus said to him, "See that you tell no one, but go show yourself to the priest, and offer the gift that Moses prescribed; that will be proof for them." MATTHEW 8:1–4

As we see in other places in the gospels, the fulfillment of the miracle wasn't in the cure, but rather in the fact that the newly healed man could demonstrate the healing to the priests and be admitted back into the community of faith and once again worship in the Temple. Communion with God and others, through healings, exorcisms, and forgiveness, seems to be the motive for much of Jesus' actions, rather than simply healing ills or doing what people wanted him to do.

Jesus also healed people and exorcised demons as a witness to his teaching authority. Miracles or signs were necessary in the ancient world to validate a preacher's message. In the Gospel of John, for example, Jesus explained, "If I do not perform my Father's works, do not believe me; but if I perform them, even if you do not believe me, believe the works, so that you may realize [and understand] that the Father is in me and I am in the Father" (John 10:37–38). The gospels of Luke and Mark seem to confirm this by indicating that Jesus' primary mission was not one of healing and fixing, but instead, preaching the good news of the Kingdom of God.[22]

The whole message of the Kingdom is a message of the loving relationship God desires to have with us and that he desires us to have with one another.[23] In order for us to grow in intimacy with one another and with God, we must let go of our false hopes that the object of our love will fix us. I have found it much more satisfying and intimate to let God *be* with me, rather than hoping God will *do* something for me!

Another popular skewed image and understanding of God is that he is the judge. Just as we can find nuances of "fixing" in the scriptural understanding of God, we can also find instances of God as the judge. However, letting God's essence be minimized to judgment negates the possibility of mutuality with him. We

---

22 Luke 4:38–44; Mark 1:35–39.

23 Matthew 22:34–40; Mark 12:28–34.

would inevitably find ourselves stuck in a spiritual life of merits and demerits where we are always fighting against failure. Rather than mutual love, our relationship with God will feel more like that of a boss and employee.

We don't have to look any further than the confessional to find the skewed image of God as the judge. Throughout my years as a priest I heard countless confessions, many of which more closely resembled a court report than a relationship with God. As such, many penitents rattled off their sins like a laundry list, never taking the time in personal prayer to truly understand their sins as merely symptoms of wounded areas in their relationship with God and others. Rather than talking to God in prayer about these relationships and growing in mutuality, they brought their list of sins before the judge hoping for clemency.

The image of God as the judge is popular because it reinforces a highly ingrained and deeply cherished American mindset. Our country was founded on the belief that individual effort is the cause of success. This has bled over into our spiritual lives. While the idea of God as the judge is not terribly appealing, most of us unconsciously love the idea of having some level of control over our salvation and a sense of being rewarded for our efforts.

Those who desire to support and maintain their skewed image of God as the judge who is weighing our righteousness and sinfulness will undoubtedly turn to Scripture verses such as Jeremiah 25:12 where God spoke through the prophet, promising, "I will punish the king of Babylon and that nation and the land of the Chaldeans for their guilt—oracle of the LORD. Their land I will turn into everlasting waste," or Jesus' words in the Gospel of John, "I came into the world for judgment" (John 9:39a).

Just as with the image of God as the fixer, Scripture invites us to read with new eyes and see the image of God shown to us through Christ. When we do this, we find a new message about judgment—it is not God who is primarily the judge, but instead, God's love manifested in word. Jesus explained this in the Gospel of John, saying, "Whoever rejects me and does not accept my words has something to judge him: the word that I spoke, it will condemn him on the last day" (John 12:48). Also, in the ministry of Christ, we find countless examples of the wonderful truth that "mercy triumphs over judgment" (James 2:13b). Jesus invites us then to "be merciful, just as your Father is merciful" (Luke 6:36).

When God is primarily our judge, we find a tangible distance between him and us. The same thing can be said for any of our unhealthy images of God, including God as the unapproachable father, abusive spouse, uncaring mother, manipulative friend, abandoner, cruel acquaintance, demanding boss, or disinterested observer. So often, these skewed images of God shape our prayer into something we *do* rather than a relationship with Someone whom we love.

For Ignatius, God was not a magician who, if cajoled the proper way, would perform a miraculous trick; nor was he a harsh judge who kept track of mistakes; nor was he a disinterested higher being who created the world and watches the drama unfold. Instead, Ignatius believed that God desires a healthy relationship with us. As such, Ignatius invites us to let go of our unhealthy images of God, much like the Israelites did thousands of years ago, and respond to the intimacy and mutuality God offers. The Jesuit priest Thomas Green explains this movement toward a healthier image in *Weeds Among the Wheat*, writing:

As time passed, however, the great religious figures of Israel began to see their relationship to Yahweh in a new light. Fatalism gave way to a sense of personal responsibility and God came to be seen as a friend and a father—a father of adult children, we might say. What I mean by this is that the father imagery is open to different interpretations depending on whether the children are young or adult. Young children are more than puppets, since they relate to their parents in love and they do have minds of their own. But they do not have the experience or the maturity to share in making the important decisions touching the family or even touching their own lives. Gradually, and usually awkwardly and painfully, they begin to assert their right to do so.[24]

Green offers us a great illustration of the mature and mutual love we find in the *Spiritual Exercises*—a relationship with God that is similar to that of an adult child and a parent. In such a relationship, we are free and able to "show reverence for all the gifts of creation and collaborate with God in using them so that by being good stewards we develop as loving persons in our care of God's world and its development." And, like adult children, we are invited—challenged—to prioritize our lives in healthy and holy ways. While this image of our relationship with God is very freeing, it can also be a bit scary.

To enter into relationship with a God whom we no longer expect or demand to fix things and to be in control (while at the same time letting go of our own control) is difficult and frightening. Most of us were taught growing up that God controls everything. Yet our experience of intimate, mutual human rela-

---

24 Green, SJ, Thomas H. *Weeds Among the Wheat*. Ave Maria Press, 1985, p. 26.

tionships, as well as what Christ taught us about the Father, challenges us to accept that God is not interested in controlling the world. At the same time, we are invited to accept that God is very interested in *being with us* no matter what we are experiencing in life. Letting God be in this role of *presence*, rather than *control*, brings great freedom to our relationship and creates the space necessary for mutual love.

Healthy images of God will always communicate his desire to be near us—a language of *presence* more than *activity*. It is an amazing freedom to no longer expect God to do things and to let prayer be an intimate sharing of our hopes, fears, desires, anxieties, struggles, and successes. Once we let go of the expectation that perfect faith and/or perfect prayer will make God do what we want him to do, we can let ourselves rest in a mutual sharing of hearts. There, we will find what our hearts most deeply desire, not a specific answer to a specific prayer, but a Person who is madly in love with us; a Lover who whispers to us:

> How beautiful you are, my friend, how beautiful you are! You are beautiful in every way, my friend, there is no flaw in you! How beautiful you are, how fair, my love. No more shall you be called "Forsaken," nor your land called "Desolate," but you shall be called "My Delight," and your land "Espoused." Though the mountains fall away and the hills be shaken, my love shall never fall away from you nor my covenant of peace be shaken. You are precious in my eyes and honored, and I love you. Remain in my love.[25]

---

25 Song of Songs 4:1, 4:7, 7:7; Isaiah 62:4, 54:10a, 43:4; John 15:9b.

Our Image of Ourselves

Years ago, I counseled a young woman who worked as a stripper. She was experiencing multiple crises in her life, including marital struggles, an unwanted pregnancy, and drug addiction. The common denominator in all of her predicaments was a profoundly skewed self-image. Deep down, she hated herself and believed that she was worthless, unlovable, and abandoned. Despite the fact that she was beautiful, intelligent, and spiritual, she considered herself trash to be discarded. This belief became a self-fulfilling prophecy as she unconsciously sabotaged relationships with family members and friends.

Over the course of many sessions, the young woman shared with me the trauma of her childhood. At the age of six, her father died of a drug overdose. Her mother also struggled with addiction and was clinically depressed. When she was in grade school, her mother would frequently tell her, "I wish I had aborted you," and when her mom bathed her she would sometimes angrily hold her head under the water in feigned attempts to drown her. All of these incidences, over the course of many years, took a toll on the young woman's self-image, ruthlessly warping it. Most of our sessions were aimed at giving God an opportunity to redefine her self-image.

Psychologists explain that each of us has a self-image, a personal view of our self that is shaped by many factors, including experiences, circumstances, and relationships. Sometimes our skewed self-image comes from viewing ourselves as particular parts—flawed parts—rather than as whole beings. At other times, it might come from our upbringing, as even the most functional childhood leaves emotional wounds. Sin, too, can be included on the list of common causes of our warped self-image, often moving our perception from "I made a mistake" to "I am a mistake," and from "I did something bad" to "I am bad."

The bottom line is that many of us have lost a deep sense of the identity God gave us. In order to grow in mutuality with God, we must grow in our self-image, seeing ourselves in the accepting and loving eyes of God. We often begin that process of healing by naming the parts of our self-image that are unhealthy. This does not necessarily require us to know the causes of our skewed self-image. Instead, we can simply name the parts of our mental self-image that are lies and then turn to God for the truth. In other words, the healthiest self-images are those that mirror God's view of us—and God's view of us is *amazing*! God created each of us to be unique, particular images of Christ for the world!

As we read in the Book of Genesis, we were made in God's image and likeness.[26] Despite the fact that we have concupiscence, or an inclination to sin, we are fundamentally good. The New Testament defines our goodness by explaining that we have been raised to the status of adopted sons and daughters of God.[27] This adoption isn't rooted in what we do or don't do, but rather in Christ's saving act on the cross, which is expressed beautifully, even poetically, by Saint Paul in his letter to the Romans when he wrote, "God proves his love for us in that while we were still sinners Christ died for us" (Romans 5:8). He did not wait for us to "get our act together," but rescued us and redeemed us simply out of love. We are *that* valuable and significant to God just as we are right now!

It took Saint Ignatius of Loyola a lifetime to understand his

---

26 Genesis 1:27.

27 Romans 8:15; Galatians 4:5; Ephesians 1:5.

inherent dignity and God's immense love for him. Throughout his life, he struggled to find a balance between an inflated view of himself and self-hate. Ignatius overcompensated for the narcissism of his youth by practicing extreme asceticism in the early years of his conversion, punishing his body through excessive mortification. As Ignatius matured, he eventually found a healthy balance that allowed him to accept that he was both loved and a sinner. He did not have to artificially inflate his self-image or squash it in false humility.

In Week One of the *Spiritual Exercises*, Ignatius invites us to pray for the grace to know that we are loved sinners, cherished by God beyond imagining. This is the balance! This is a healthy self-image! We neither have to narcissistically negate our sins and struggles nor beat ourselves up for every misstep and failure. Instead, we can accept ourselves as loved and cherished by God as his blessed daughters and sons. Coming to accept such a grace is not easy; it requires a lot of relational prayer time, letting go of our false selves, and meditating and contemplating from a place of poverty rather than a place of certitude. In such surrender and emptiness, we find the space to let God be God and let ourselves be the unique, particular image of Christ that God created us to be.

Sin

One of the noticeable differences between most young people and older folks is that the former care what others think about how they dress, and the latter don't seem to care much at all. When we're young we spend copious amounts of time and energy making sure that we look and dress appropriately for the various situations in our lives. For example, a mother was relating to me that her teenage daughter called all of her friends repeatedly in order to verify that "everyone" was going to wear leggings on a recent bus trip. As we get older, we find ourselves caring less and less, or maybe we just don't have the energy and time it takes to verify everyone else's opinions. We desire to spend our time focused on things more important than looking good for others.

Something very similar happens in our spiritual lives. When we are spiritual neophytes, we spend a lot of time and energy trying to "look good" to God. We tend to define holiness as the absence of sin and, therefore, we willfully and sometimes violently try to rip sin out of our lives. Yet we usually find the fruit of this approach to be superficial, producing temporary "successes" and lasting frustrations. Our hyper-focus on sins often leads us to mistakenly equate our sins with our true identity. We feel like we have nothing to bring to God unless we can fix ourselves and get "cleaned up." I saw this frequently in the sacrament of reconciliation. Penitents often only confessed the sins that they had seemingly conquered, saying things like, "Well, I used to drink too much, but I quit doing that a few weeks ago." Such subtleties expose our desire to approach God only when we are "good enough."

This is precisely the obstacle that sin is to mutual love with God. In our spiritual beginnings we often fall for the trap that we can only be intimate with God if we are perfect. As I mentioned earlier, Saint Paul addressed this lie when he wrote, "God proves his love for us in that *while we were still sinners* Christ died for us" (Romans 5:8 [*emphasis mine*]). Mutuality with God, according to Ignatius, is a sharing of goods and selves. God does not ask us to only share what is perfect, but to share everything. Jesus offered a beautiful parable that illustrates this important point:

[Jesus] proposed another parable to them. "The kingdom of heaven may be likened to a man who sowed good seed in his field. While everyone was asleep his enemy came and sowed weeds all through the wheat, and then went off. When the crop grew and bore fruit, the weeds appeared as well. The slaves of the householder came to him and said, 'Master, did you not sow good seed in your field? Where have the weeds come from?' He answered, 'An enemy has done this.' His slaves said to him, 'Do you want us to go and pull them up?' He replied, 'No, if you pull up the weeds you might uproot the wheat along with them. Let them grow together until harvest; then at harvest time I will say to the harvesters, "First collect the weeds and tie them in bundles for burning; but gather the wheat into my barn."'" MATTHEW 13:24–30

This parable is not about some abstract "kingdom of heaven" that is *out there*; it is about the human heart. Each and every one of us possesses both weeds and wheat. Satan or, as Saint Ignatius of Loyola calls him, "the enemy of our human nature," sows seeds of weeds in us through our woundedness and sin. Yet God has created us to be good, and no matter how much sinfulness we find in ourselves, the field of our lives is made for and contains the wheat of God's goodness and love.

This is an image of great gentleness and acceptance. It invites us beyond the language of "either I'm sinful or I'm holy" and into the language of "I am both sinful and holy," a loved sinner. It is a movement from spiritual immaturity to spiritual maturity. As we make that journey, we find ourselves focusing less and less on the weeds and trusting more and more in God's love and mercy. We realize that it is not so much our individual sins that keep us from mutuality with God; it is instead our feelings of sinfulness and not being "good enough." Thankfully, suffering, humility, love, and prayer facilitate the spiritual growth necessary to lead us to see our sinfulness as a paradoxical blessing that allows us to set aside *our* definition of holiness (i.e., the absence of sin) and accept *Christ's* definition of holiness—love. Then, mutuality with God deepens, and without falling into the sin of presumption,[28] we share everything with God—our entire selves, the weeds and the wheat.

Anger

While anger and egoism are often sinful, I would be remiss in simply lumping them with the section above on sin, because we experience them so distinctly. For example, anger is the most recognizable and feel-able emotion we have as human beings. And it is not always sinful; even Jesus got angry. However, after years of doing pastoral counseling and spiritual direction with people, I've come to believe that one of the most common blocks to mutuality with God is our anger at him. The reason why it is so toxic is because many of us have been led to believe that anger at God is inappropriate. As such, we become spiritually stuck. If mutuality is sharing our entire selves with God, but we don't want to share the anger we feel at him, then we will unconsciously keep ourselves at a comfortable distance. The irony, of course, is that God *already knows* how we feel! We are not hiding anything from him by not sharing our anger with him.

Great freedom comes when we accept that God is expansive enough to hold our anger. Rather than telling him what we think

28 Romans 6:1.

he wants to hear, we are free to share with him everything, including our anger. Sharing our anger with God is a place of great intimacy, and it usually leads to new and deeper insights into our anger and the situations that led to our anger. This is why Saint Augustine believed that we do not pray in order to share with God what he already knows, but to increase our desire for God and our capacity to receive his response to us.[29] That is mutual love and intimacy.

Ego

One day in college seminary, one of my friends dropped by my dorm room. I could tell when he walked in that he was sad and angry. When I asked him what was wrong he explained that he had just come from his annual review by the seminary faculty. He said that the review was mostly positive, but the faculty indicated that he needed to grow in humility. He looked me straight in the eye and ironically bragged, "They're crazy! I'm the humblest person in the world!" I started to laugh, assuming that he was joking, but he was not.

The ego is a powerful energy in our lives. Like anger, the ego is not necessarily bad, but it can become a block to mutual love. In order to reverence its role in our lives while not being constantly manipulated by it, we must grow in our understanding of the ego. It is generally understood to be the part of our psyche that judges, tests, plans, defends, creates boundaries, defines reality, and synthesizes information. It's not something inherently bad, but in order for us to be healthy, the ego must play its part without trying to be all of the parts.

---

29 Augustine of Hippo, Letter 130.

We have all experienced and been the recipients of the anger and dysfunction of an unhealthy, out-of-control ego. In his book *Everything Belongs*, Richard Rohr explains the experience, writing,

> [Egotistical] people...are, frankly, very difficult to live with. Every one of their ego-boundaries must be defended, negotiated, or worshiped: their reputation, their needs, their nation, their security, their religion, even their ball team. They convince themselves that these boundaries are all they have to worry about because they are the sum-total of their identity.[30]

An unchecked ego negatively impacts our spiritual growth by increasing our desire to be in control, willful, independent, self-sufficient, blameless, and guiltless. Such drives are contrary to mutuality. Instead, mutual love is marked with surrender, willingness, interdependence, reliance, gentleness, and responsibility. As such, those who have the courage to embrace love, suffering, and prayer will find the grip of their ego loosening and a growing capacity for mutuality with God and others.

Recognizing the ways in which our egos are out of control is relatively easy but almost always painful; therefore, we usually opt to live in ignorance. Those who courageously decide to take a long, honest gaze at their ego find that it operates in very distinct ways, which primarily manifest through excessive emotions toward people or situations. The simple gauge is for us to be aware of when our emotional reaction is greater than what the person or situation warrants. A couple of examples will help illustrate my point.

----

30 "Center and Circumference." The Crossroad Publishing Company, 2003.

I found myself very irritated by a man who talked too much. I tried to avoid him as much as possible. When I was forced to be around him, I no longer cared about *what* he said, but was preoccupied with *how much* he said. My emotional reaction to his rambling was far greater than what the situation logically warranted. As I took my irritation to prayer, I realized that there was more to the situation than the old adage, "What I hate about him, I hate about myself."

Instead, I realized that my ego worshipped the idol of "being an entertaining narrator." Every time I heard him speak and realized that people were not entertained by the stories he shared, I was forced to acknowledge that my idol might be false. In other words, if *he* was not an entertaining narrator, maybe *I* wasn't either. If *his* golden idol of talking was a sham, maybe *mine* was too. It was much easier to avoid him rather than confront the ways in which I try to get people's attention through the stories I share.

When we feel irritated, it's almost always connected to our overactive ego. I remember being irritated with a friend from school. Unconsciously, I had classified her as spiritually immature—a spiritual neophyte—and I found myself irritated by her attempts to get people to affirm her perceived spiritual maturity. I tried to rationalize and justify the ways in which she irritated me, but in the end, I was forced to acknowledge that she was merely a reminder that my ego worshipped the false idol of my own "spiritual maturity." I came to realize that I had slowly, over the course of many years, built my identity on being "spiritually mature." Rather than being angry with her, I was invited to melt the "golden calf" of spiritual superiority in my own life.

What irritates us the most in life, then, will often be the false idols in other people's lives that force us to acknowledge our own false idols. It is precisely the ego that tries to manage and maintain those false idols and images. As you can imagine, anything false is clearly a block to mutuality. It would be analogous to going to meet a friend in a costume, which would provide a level of obscurity to our true identity.

Unforgiveness

I tend to fall asleep within seconds of my head hitting the pillow. I remember one particular night, however, when that did not happen, and I lay there feeling overwhelmed. I grabbed my rosary and tried to pray, but I couldn't even do something so simple. I finally got out of bed and plopped down in my prayer chair and asked God what was going on. I let myself just feel...and what I felt was anger. As I sat with the anger, I began noticing that it wasn't anger as much as deep betrayal. I felt betrayed. I immediately realized that I had been carrying unforgiveness in my heart toward a friend whom I felt had betrayed me a few days earlier. As I sat with that particular instance of betrayal, I realized that there was a deeper betrayal underneath it.

Three months earlier, a few priests with whom I was close betrayed me. I had unconsciously pushed the feelings of betrayal and anger deep down into my heart and ignored them until they became unforgiveness. That night, as I sat in my prayer chair, I decided it was time to let it go. I gave myself permission to fully and completely feel the betrayal and sobbed for forty-five minutes, hoping for the courage to forgive them. Eventually, the courage came, and I forgave each of them out loud in prayer. I felt a great peace, like the weight of the world was lifted off of my shoulders. It was a beautiful reminder of the enslaving, disquieting, and toxic nature of unforgiveness and of the freeing, peaceful, and mutual nature of forgiveness.

We come to understand how unforgiveness can be an obstacle to our mutuality with God only when we understand that our relationship with God is intimately connected to our relationship with others. In other words, the separateness we experience when we're unwilling to forgive another person becomes separateness in our relationship with God. When we are unwilling to share all of ourselves—including our forgiveness—with others, then we are also withholding part of ourselves from God.

It takes a tremendous amount of prayer and spiritual maturity for us to understand and experience this level of connectedness between our relationship with others and our relationship with God. It takes even more prayer and spiritual maturity to realize that the limitless forgiveness that Christ calls us to offer others is not the same as forgetting who and what hurt us, or continually allowing ourselves to be hurt or abused.

Fear

A popular term in spiritual direction ministry is "resistance," which refers to a directee's reluctance to pray about or talk about a particular aspect of his or her relationship with God. As you can imagine, this is an obstacle to intimacy with God. When we are reluctant to talk with our Beloved about a particular subject, we are withholding a part of ourselves. Rarely is such resistance done maliciously or on purpose. In fact, we are often not even aware that we're being resistant until it's discovered through prayer or spiritual direction.

Over the years I've come to realize that all resistance is rooted in fear. Sometimes our fear is quickly discoverable and easily worked through. This was the case with a man whom I directed years ago. During one of our sessions he explained to me that God had been very silent during his personal prayer times. I asked him, "What is the silence like?" He avoided answering the question for about thirty minutes before he realized his resistance. His awareness led to an amazing discovery as he said, "I've been avoiding answering your question! I don't want to answer because deep down I fear that the silence is God's displeasure with me." Wow! By recognizing his resistance and naming the fear, he was able to experience a great freedom to talk to God about the perceived displeasure.

Sometimes, our fears can be so overwhelmingly powerful that they cause us to become spiritually and emotionally catatonic or cause us to flee to false consolations. Often, these deep fears exist in many layers. For example, over the course of many months of spiritual direction, one courageous directee was able to name deeper and deeper fears. What began with "I don't like other people" became "I fear being used by others." As more months of spiritual direction sessions unfolded, she heard herself say, "I fear being hurt" and then, "I fear falling in love." Still, we were not down to her deepest fears. As layers were peeled back, she was finally able to acknowledge, "I fear vulnerability" and "I fear not being good enough." It takes tremendous courage and grace to face our fears, but doing so is clearly a path to deeper mutuality with God, a more complete sharing of ourselves.

The list of common fears that come up in our spiritual lives is quite long and includes the fear of being unlovable, fear of what God might ask of us, fear of failure, fear of vulnerability, fear of not being good enough, fear of being abandoned, fear of being alone, fear of not having enough, fear of being unforgivable, fear of surrendering, fear of accepting, and fear of death. Regardless of the fear, it's important for each of us, like the man and woman mentioned above, to recognize our resistance and let it lead us to—and through—our fears. Listed below are some of the common signs of resistance that can occur during our prayer time; they help us to know we have bumped into the obstacle of fear. While no single one of these signs definitively indicates that we are reluctant to acknowledge our fear, patterns and persistency in them often do.

- Being overly self-preoccupied
- Having an emotionally unnuanced experience of prayer
- Saying or praying the same thing, over and over
- Frequently falling asleep in prayer
- Avoiding prayer
- Doing a lot of spiritual reading during prayer
- Busying ourselves with distractions during prayer
- Telling God what we think he wants to hear
- Ignoring our feelings during prayer
- Starting prayer time late
- Ending prayer time early

Clutter

I remember the first time I visited the home of a hoarder. I was shocked, but I tried to hide it as I shuffled sideways, navigating from the front door to her living room. She was clearly embarrassed, and I knew my shock would only add to her embarrassment. Yet I honestly wanted to ask, "How did this happen?" While I didn't feel comfortable asking the woman that question, I asked God in prayer the next morning, and rather than focusing on the stuffed house I visited the previous day, God began to show me the clutter in my own life.

As Americans, most of us live in utter clutter. We willingly participate in a culture of excess. Our lives are filled with various forms of clutter that preoccupy our time and energy and hinder our intimacy with God. Like the clutter in a hoarder's home, the clutter in our lives is an obstacle to sharing our goods and ourselves fully with God. Depending on the manifestation of the clutter, it impacts our mutual love with God in varying ways and degrees. Here are some of the manifestations of clutter that I've become cognizant of in my own life.

Busyness is a form of clutter. In the Gospel of Luke (10:38–42), Jesus explained to Martha how her busyness was clutter. We are all familiar with this story. Mary sat at Jesus' feet listening to him while Martha busied herself with hospitality. When Martha complained to Jesus, His response was, "Martha, Martha, you are anxious and worried about many things. There is need of only one thing. Mary has chosen the better part and it will not be taken from her."

The clutter of busyness can be clearly seen by looking at our calendars and to-do lists. Take for example the calendars of parents with children. Many of these parents have shared with me their frustration in trying to juggle their children's numerous activities. The fear of not being a good enough parent and not letting their children do what other children get to do leads these parents to run from one event to another without time to reflect on the experiences or share with God what the experiences mean.

One does not have to be a parent of small children to be busy, though. People of all ages and walks of life have told me that the number one reason they don't pray regularly is because they are too busy. Since our personal prayer time is the heart of our relationship with God and not another calendar event to "get done," being too busy to pray is an obstacle to deepening mutuality with God. Instead, God says to us, "*Be still* and know that I am God" (Psalm 46:11a [*emphasis mine*]).

Noise is also a form of clutter. For prayer to move from a monologue to a dialogue, we must take time to be quiet and listen. The more we surround ourselves with background noise throughout the day, the harder it is to enter into quiet listening during prayer. The clutter of noise might include having the TV going even when no one is watching, listening to the radio every time we're in the car, playing music when we invite friends to the house, or incessant small talk. Gently quieting the clutter of noise in our lives will open up new opportunities for God to speak to us and for us to speak to God.

Material possessions can also be clutter, even for non-hoarders. Jesus spoke frequently about the dangers of riches and possessions. For example, in the Gospel of Matthew (19:16–24), Jesus was blessing some children when a young man approached and asked, "Teacher, what good must I do to gain eternal life?" When Jesus explained that the young man should not only keep the commandments, but also sell all of his possessions, give the money to the poor, and follow him, the young man "went away sad, for he had many possessions." Jesus used the opportunity to tell his Apostles, "Amen, I say to you, it will be hard for one who is rich to enter the kingdom of heaven. Again I say to you, it is easier for a camel to pass through the eye of a needle than for one who is rich to enter the kingdom of God."

Money and most possessions are amoral; they are neither good nor bad. Jesus' point, then, is that our lives should not be so cluttered with possessions that they limit our freedom and become an obstacle to a deeper relationship with God. I remember when I was in college seminary and my brother bought me a VCR. That was a huge moment for a nineteen-year-old with no money! I enjoyed inviting friends to my dorm room to watch movies. As the weeks passed, I found myself ruminating more and more about the safety of my VCR. I worried about whether I had locked my door before leaving for class and worried about someone stealing it. I was reluctant to let others borrow it for fear that it would get damaged. It didn't take long for me to realize that I didn't own the VCR; it owned me. That possession limited my freedom and unnecessarily consumed my energy and thoughts. That is a sign that our possessions have become clutter.

There are countless things that can become obstacles to our mutuality with God. However, we trust that God's grace will help us. He desires nothing more than to gently draw us around those obstacles and into deeper intimacy through relational prayer, which I cover in the next chapter.

REFLECTION QUESTIONS

1. How has your image of God changed throughout your life?

2. How has your image of yourself changed?

3. What image of God has provided you with the greatest freedom to grow in love with him?

4. What obstacles stand in the way of growing in intimacy with your closest human friend? What graces would you need in order to move through those obstacles?

5. What obstacles stand in the way of greater intimacy, mutuality, transparency, and vulnerability with God? What graces would you need in order to move through those obstacles?

6. When have you been the angriest at God, and why? What did you do with that anger? How did God respond to the anger?

7. Who are the people who most irritate you, and why? Can you name which of your "idols" they are making a mockery of through their irritating personality?

8. How do you see your ego manifested the most clearly?

9. Whom have you struggled the most to forgive? Why?

10. What do you fear? When you peel back the layers of fear what do you discover?

11. Name the greatest clutter in your life. What grace would you need in order to de-clutter that part of your life?

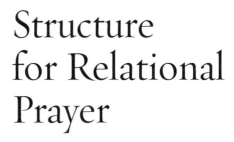

CHAPTER FIVE

Structure for Relational Prayer

Christine was noticeably nervous when she walked into my spiritual direction office for the first time. She had never been to spiritual direction before and wasn't sure what to expect. After an opening prayer, I invited her to share with me the story of her spiritual journey. She spent the next thirty minutes sharing with me what it was like attending a small Baptist church in rural Arkansas and the numerous ways in which she had experienced God's presence, love, and mercy. She shared with me the people who had been instrumental in shaping her character and spirituality. When she finished, I asked her the question I ask all of my new directees, "How would you describe your personal prayer time?"

Christine's answer to my question was similar to most of my new directees. She described her personal prayer as mainly intercessory, talking to God about the needs of particular people and situations, and asking God for help. Additionally, Christine was not content with the structure of her prayer time. Like the structure of most people's prayer time, it was not very relational. It consisted of some daily Scripture readings and reflections from various websites, apps, and books. Christine desired something more, something deeper, and she is not alone.

There seems to be a growing desire in people of all religions and denominations for a deeper, more relational, connection to God. In this chapter, I offer a structure for relational, personal prayer that addresses that collective desire. The structure is comprised of recommendations from Ignatius of Loyola, as well as practices that I've found helpful in my own prayer life. The following suggestions are not meant to be an exact recipe to follow in order to feel like our prayer is successful; rather, they are suggestions that have helped many people, like Christine, deepen the relationality of their personal prayer and experience the intimacy they desire. Here is an overview of that structure:

1. Reverence the presence of God
2. Review yesterday's prayer
3. Ask for the grace you most deeply desire
4. Meditate on the desire
5. Invite others into the conversation
6. Review the prayer time and then journal

Not only do I encourage you to try the recommendations and use the ones that bear good spiritual fruit, but I also encourage you to pay attention to how they are operative not only in your relationship with God, but also in your intimate human relationships. In fact, I'll use the story of Matt and Sandy's engagement to illustrate this connectedness and the structure for relational prayer.

Reverence the Presence of God

One of my favorite moments in preparing couples for marriage is inviting them to share with me the story of their engagement. When I asked Matt and Sandy to share their engagement story with me, their eyes lit up and they both smiled. Sandy began the story by explaining that Matt had invited her to his apartment for wine and then they were going to go out for dinner. When Sandy arrived, she discovered that Matt had cleaned his apartment, placed vanilla-scented candles around the living room, prepared *hors d'oeuvres*, and opened a bottle of her favorite white wine. When I asked her how she felt when she saw all of the preparation he had done for her, she responded that she felt welcomed, accepted, and cherished.

Our personal prayer begins in a similar way. We are encouraged to have a special place prepared for prayer. Ideally, it is a place that is free of clutter and distractions; a place that is quiet and one that is different from where we do other, more mundane, things. For some people, this is a special prayer chair in the corner of a room, near their Bible and prayer journal. For others, this special space is an entire room dedicated to prayer, reflection, and reading. Regardless of the amount of space we can dedicate in our homes for meditation, God is pleased with the room we make for him; it is sacred ground, and it becomes a special place we are excited to visit each day.

In addition to creating a welcoming atmosphere for God, we are invited to reverence his presence. Just as Matt welcomed Sandy at the beginning of their date, we should welcome God at the beginning of our personal prayer time. While this might seem obvious, the truth is that many people begin prayer without ever acknowledging God's presence and love. In the insane busyness of our lives, it is so easy to become task-oriented and fail to reverence the presence of others. If we take a moment to remember yesterday, I bet most of us can think of at least one example of how we became so hyper-focused on a task that we ignored people or God. It happens to me frequently.

I remember one day as I walked through the office, I saw a woman standing at the receptionist's desk. Our eyes met for a moment, and I offered a half-hearted smile and continued walking to the copy machine. I was in a hurry to get copies made for the class I was teaching that evening. Later, as I was sitting at my desk, the image of the woman's eyes flashed in my mind and I was shocked by the grief I saw! I had been so preoccupied with finishing the photocopies that I missed *really seeing* the woman.

I quickly buzzed the receptionist and asked if the woman was still there, but she had already left. The receptionist shared with me that the woman had come to the office to find out the steps she needed to take to plan the funeral for her recently deceased father. My heart sank. In my busyness, I had missed an opportunity to reverence the presence of one of God's children. Just as I frequently miss opportunities to reverence the presence of others, I sometimes miss the opportunity to reverence the presence of God at the beginning of personal prayer.

It is easy for me to be ten or fifteen minutes into my prayer time before realizing that I never consciously acknowledged

God's presence and love. Clearly, I'm not the only person who has struggled with such distractions and busyness, because Saint Ignatius, in paragraph seventy-five of his *Spiritual Exercises*, recommends that we begin our prayer time by reverencing God's presence and his loving gaze in some concrete and conscious way.

> A step or two before the place where I am to contemplate or meditate, I will stand for the space of an Our Father, and with my consciousness raised on high, I will consider how the Lord my God beholds me. Then I will make an act of reverence or humility.

Ignatius is not recommending that we actually start with the Lord's Prayer, but that we take a moment—roughly the amount of time it would take to pray the Lord's Prayer—to recollect ourselves, acknowledging God's presence and love. This simple and short practice helps us move from busyness and doing to intimacy and being. It helps us shift from task-orientation to God-orientation. It helps us move from the countless Martha-like demands of life to an opportunity to be Mary, sitting at the feet of Jesus.[31] It is, in essence, our welcoming God and God welcoming us, just as Matt welcomed Sandy.

Review Yesterday's Prayer

As Matt took over telling their engagement story, he explained that, while they sipped Chardonnay, he asked Sandy where she wanted to go for dinner. Rather than getting a simple and clear answer from her, she began reminiscing about the restaurants where they had recently dined. Matt explained to me that he was

---

31 Luke 10:38–42.

expecting a quick answer, but Sandy put much more thought into it. She was figuring out where she wanted to eat based on what she was craving and what recent cravings she had satiated. I could sense Matt's frustration as he told this part of the story, despite the months that had passed. Sandy playfully defended herself by explaining that she takes dining very seriously.

Just as Sandy seemed incapable of naming her craving without first remembering past cravings, I have found that it is really important for us to remember previous topics of conversation with God before we can name the topic we currently desire to discuss during personal prayer. In this way, conversations, like relationships, should have a natural flow and development. When they don't, life can be awkward and painful. This was precisely the premise of the 2004 movie *50 First Dates* starring Adam Sandler and Drew Barrymore.

The movie plot involves a young woman named Lucy, played by Barrymore, who suffered from memory loss due to a car accident. Every day she woke up believing it was October 13. Every night when she slept, the day's events vanished from her memory. Because of her condition, a smitten young man named Henry, played by Sandler, struggled to move their relationship forward. It took tremendous energy, planning, and suffering in order for Henry to move their relationship beyond the same-old conversation and the same-old level of relationship as the previous day.

Thankfully, we do not have to exert nearly as much energy, planning, and suffering in order to keep our conversation and relationship with God moving forward. One of the most helpful tools for deepening and developing our communication with God is simply reviewing the previous day's prayer time and prayer journal entry. In doing so, we remember our previous conversation with God so as to continue to develop that topic of conversation. In this way, we don't have to start back at square one each day.

I cannot overestimate the importance of this step in personal prayer. Many of my new directees describe their prayer as being like a rock skipping across water, staying superficial and disconnected; each day they skip from one topic to the next, never letting their conversation with God sink deepwardly. They approach prayer as if they have amnesia about the previous day's prayer. One day they might ask God to help a friend, the next day they might pray for the gift of patience, and the following day they might play "Bible roulette," flipping it open and reading whatever passage they see. Thankfully, there is a healthier way!

By reviewing our previous day's prayer, we reverence where the "rock" of conversation is, and we let it slow down and sink deeper, rather than prematurely skipping to a new topic. Prayer becomes very relational and personal when we stay with particular topics and conversations for days, weeks, and even months.

How long should we continue a particular conversation and topic of prayer with God? Saint John of the Cross offers us a beautiful image of encouragement, depth, and perseverance, writing, "We must dig deeply in Christ. He is like a rich mine with many pockets containing treasures: however deep we dig we will never find their end or their limit. Indeed, in every pocket new seams of fresh riches are discovered on all sides."[32] In other words, we continue sharing with God the deepest desire of our heart, exploring every "new seam" until we are certain that we've exhausted the conversation and we find the desire of our heart, the topic of conversation, has changed.

---

32 John of the Cross, Prayer from a Canticle.

Ask for the Grace You Most Deeply Desire

Having reverenced the presence of God and remembered the topic of conversation we were having with him, Ignatius invites us to name the grace we most deeply desire. In paragraph forty-eight of the *Spiritual Exercises*, he writes, "I will ask God our Lord for what I want and desire." That desire, which can be a spiritual gift or topic of conversation, will normally be intimately connected to the previous graces we've recently written down in our prayer journal. Just like a deep craving for Mexican food will keep us going from one Mexican restaurant to the next until the craving is satiated, our deepest spiritual desires will keep the topic of conversation consistent and ongoing until that desire transforms into a new one. Sandy experienced that same truth in her food cravings.

As Matt continued the story of their engagement, it became clear that Sandy had exhausted her craving for Mexican food, remembering that the last four restaurants they had dined at were Mexican. She told Matt that she was craving something new and different—Italian. Matt had heard about a great new Italian restaurant downtown that would be the perfect atmosphere for the proposal he had planned. Just as Sandy's craving gave direction to their date, when you and I name our heart's deepest desire, it gives direction to our personal prayer time.

The idea of anchoring our personal prayer in our heart's deepest desire is new for many people. Often, when I ask directees to name their deepest desire, they feel overwhelmed. Many of them find it helpful for me to reframe the request using an image of Christ visiting them. I ask them, "If Jesus came in and sat down right beside you and explained that he only had fifteen minutes to spend with you, what would you want to talk to him about?"

I explain to them that their answer, in order to keep it relational, cannot entail prayers for other people or situations.

This image seems to provide many of them with a new clarity about their answer. They express concise desires like "I want to be more loving," "I desire to be more patient," "I hope to finally forgive my mom," "I want to experience new freedom," and "I want to grow in trusting God." Finding concise desires like these is not always easy. It might require us to peel back layers of feelings within our hearts. That is exactly what my friend James learned.

James shared with me an experience he had of peeling back layers of feelings in order to name his deepest desire. He explained that at the beginning of his prayer time he felt distracted and unsettled. He tried to concentrate on the prayer app that he used each morning, but he continued feeling restless. Finally, he set the app aside and acknowledged what he was feeling.

At first, he only recognized and named the restlessness, but the longer he sat with it, the more he realized that he felt agitated. Knowing that agitation is often just a fancy word for anger, he acknowledged his anger. This helped him to ask the question, "Who or what am I angry at?" He immediately remembered a conversation he had the previous day with his wife. During the conversation she dismissed his opinion, saying that it was ridiculous. He realized that under his anger he felt deeply hurt by her dismissive comment. Then, and only then, was James able to name his desire to forgive his wife and better understand her opinion. The restlessness vanished, and James was able to enjoy a beautiful conversation with God about his desire.

This is a great example of the importance of peeling back the layers of affect in order to name what is truly stirring in our hearts. When we do, we will be able to more clearly name our heart's deepest desire and know what topic of conversation we should have with God. In addition to providing us with a topic for meditation, naming our deepest desire also focuses our listening. Most of us have witnessed such focused listening from the mothers of newborns.

Imagine a mother of a newborn working at the desk of her home office. The washing machine is running, the dryer is on, the dishwasher is loudly scouring dirty dishes, and the television is running in the living room. Yet, when her newborn makes the slightest cry, she hears and responds. How can she hear the child with all of that background noise? It's because her newborn daughter is the most important thing to her—she is her heart's deepest desire! Psychologists call this phenomenon "selective attention" and tell us that we are most inclined to hear and see what we desire to hear and see.

Daniel Simons and Christopher Chabris became famous for their research on selective attention. They produced an experiment titled "The Invisible Gorilla" in which viewers were asked to count the number of times basketball players dressed in white passed the ball to one another. As the three players in white passed the ball, they continuously moved around in a small circle with three players dressed in black. The majority of viewers were so focused on counting the passes that they completely missed the man in the gorilla suit who walked through the small circle of players. How could they miss something so obvious? Selective attention!

By naming our heart's deepest desire, we help to narrow the voices of the countless distractions that float around in our minds and hearts each day. We find ourselves more focused to hear the voice of God in the midst of all those other voices. Just as Sandy narrowed the number of possible restaurants by naming her

desire for Italian, we pinpoint a special conversation with God
when we name our heart's deepest desire. Conversely, when we
don't take the time to discern the most important movement of
our hearts and to name our deepest desire, we will usually hop
from one topic to the next and from one distraction to the next
during prayer.

Meditate on the Desire

Once we've named our deepest desire—the most important conversation we want to have with God—we are ready to bring it to
personal prayer and let it draw us into intimacy with God. While
it might seem like this would be an easy part of personal prayer,
most of my directees agree that it's the hardest. Sometimes they
are able to name the deep desire of their heart but are unable to
figure out how to savor that desire in personal prayer. It would be
like Sandy knowing what kind of food she was craving but being
unable to choose an Italian restaurant.

Before I get into the details of how to savor and meditate on
our deepest desires, it's important to make a distinction between
meditation and contemplation. While various authors have
defined meditation and contemplation in very different ways, I
define meditation as prayer that involves an *object of focus*, while
contemplation has no object of focus. In other words, our meditation might include an object of focus like sacred Scripture, a
poem, a quote from a favorite book, a sound, a favorite song, a
mantra, a painting or picture, a thought or memory, a smell or
a texture. These tangible experiences help to draw us into conversation with God much like watching a movie together might
provide two friends with a topic of conversation. In my definition
of contemplative prayer, there is no object of focus; instead, we

quietly sit, being present to God without letting our minds be captured by thoughts.

In this particular step of relational prayer, I focus on meditation rather than contemplation. Neither form of prayer is better than the other, but meditation is definitely the more popular practice of personal prayer. As we look for ways to meditate on our deepest desire, then, I recommend that we do two things— be creative and enjoy! Prayer does not need to be boring or mundane. In fact, there is no greater way to create a nonnegotiable habit of personal prayer each day than to ensure our prayer is rooted in our deepest desire and is creative and enjoyable!

Just as Sandy's craving for Italian food might have lasted for months and might have led her and Matt to visit numerous different Italian restaurants, our deepest desire can manifest itself in numerous styles of meditation that help us continue our conversation with God. For example, we might use imaginative prayer, the prayer of consideration, *lectio divina*, or *visio divina* with the object of our meditation being a Scripture story, picture, song, memory, etc. Ultimately, the object of our meditation and the style of our meditation are less important than their power to draw us into an encounter with God.

As we meditate, we share with God what it is stirring up in our hearts—the desires and affective movements. We give God opportunities to speak to us through the object of our meditation. The conversation continues until our prayer time ends. The point of the conversation is not to convince God to do something for us but to simply let God get to know us and for us to get to know God. If we approach this special time of prayer with thoughts like "God already knows me" or "I can't get to know God," then we shut down the intimacy of relationship. Instead, we vulnerably open ourselves up, sharing with God what is most important and letting him share with us. I experienced this intimacy in important ways while building my spiritual direction ministry.

As I began a full-time spiritual direction ministry, I desired to learn more about mission statements and wanted to write one with Jesus. For weeks, my personal prayer time was spent talking to Jesus about what a mission statement is and how it could help me to stay focused on what was most important in my ministry.

For several days, I used Scripture passages that helped me better understand the core qualities and values that directed Jesus' decisions and mission. I wrote his values in my prayer journal and then shared with him my own core qualities and values. I really enjoyed those conversations with Christ and found myself looking forward to continuing the topic each morning in prayer. Eventually, he and I wrote a mission statement for DeepWardly Spiritual Direction Services. We then moved on to learning about vision statements and writing one of those, as well.

As I think about those prayer times and write about them now, I find myself smiling and feeling the contentment that came from those special times with Jesus. It ended up being about so much more than just writing a mission statement and vision statement; it was intimate time with Jesus, getting to know him and sharing myself with him. I experienced the consolation of Christ's interest in my ministry and his gratitude for my service.

While that particular example of relational prayer involved me using Scripture passages for meditation, we can meditate on other things as well. For example, I once used a painting of the Trinity to meditate on the suffering I was experiencing. This was during a particularly dark time in my life and in my spiritual journey. I was in Week Three of the *Spiritual Exercises*, where I found myself every day in prayer simply being with Jesus in his suffering and enduring the agony.

One morning in prayer, after expressing my desire to continue to be with Christ in his suffering, I felt restless. After struggling to stay focused, I decided to visualize where I was in the Passion narrative. In my innermost spirit I knew that in my spiritual journey with Christ, he had been taken off the cross but had not yet been placed in the tomb. I searched the internet for images of Christ's Passion and, as I slowly scrolled through them, one image jumped off the iPad screen. It was an image of the Father holding the crucified and limp body of Jesus while the Holy Spirit was descending upon him.

I used a style of meditation called the "prayer of consideration" with the image, letting God speak to me through details of the painting. As the prayer time unfolded, my heart was led to the hands of God, and I realized that the Father was taking the crown of thorns off Jesus' head. Immediately, I realized that I was in a transition out of the particular suffering I was experiencing in Week Three. My spirit felt settled and peaceful. I found myself filled with new hope and encouragement. I ended prayer by journaling about the experience.

These two examples illustrate the structure I recommend for personal prayer in order to keep it relational. They entail all of the steps I've mentioned so far, as well as creatively choosing an object for meditation. Since the most common struggle in relational prayer seems to be finding objects for meditation, I have provided numerous pages of helpful suggestions in the appendix of this book. In fact, I've taken some of the most common desires that people name and have provided numerous Scripture passages and creative ideas for how we could spend prayer meditating on those desires. I hope those ideas and suggestions stir up your own creativity and desire for relational prayer.

Invite Others into the Conversation

Matt's smile was contagious as he described getting down on one knee at the Italian restaurant and proposing to Sandy. He was clearly proud of himself and madly in love with Sandy, who listened intently to his description of that special moment. When he finished, she quickly picked up the story, detailing her announcement to her family. She smiled just as broadly as she described showing the ring to her parents and sharing her joy with them. It was clear to me that their engagement was too significant to keep secret; they chose to share their joy with family and friends.

Saint Ignatius believed that our relationship with God is something so special and important that we need to share it with others, even during prayer. Ignatius had a special prayer technique for doing this, which he called the "colloquy." We might think about the colloquy as a conversation with a member of the Trinity or with a saint. Ignatius invites us to talk to one of these persons as though we were having a casual conversation with a friend.

Just as we go to multiple friends to get their thoughts and opinions on important matters and to share special events and news with them, we do this spiritually and prayerfully through the colloquy. For example, having talked with Jesus about his core qualities and values, and how those helped define his mission, I talked to Saint Ignatius of Loyola and reflected on his core qualities and values and how they defined his mission. Ignatius' qualities, mission, and life help me to better understand Christ's mission as well as my own. This is the gift of the colloquy.

One of my directees expressed to me his desire to become a teacher. In addition to reflecting on Scripture passages that highlighted Christ's role as a teacher—a rabbi—he also learned about Saint John Bosco, the patron saint of teachers, and talked to him about what made him an outstanding teacher. Outside of prayer, he read books about Saint John and learned more about his style of teaching and his desire to serve, which gave him additional material to talk to Jesus about during prayer. In this way, the colloquy enriched his prayer time and helped him to experience a solidarity with others who loved teaching.

An important aspect of the colloquy is that it reminds us of our interconnectedness with others. It doesn't take anything away from our relationship with Christ, but it reminds us that we are members of the body of Christ. All of the men and women who have gone before us in faith continue to be members of the body of Christ; they continue to be our brothers and sisters in Christ. The colloquy helps us to savor the gift of those important relationships in our spiritual family. Just as Sandy wanted to share her good news with her family and get their response and reaction, we can share our deepest desires with the members of our spiritual family and be blessed by their response, example, and encouragement.

The colloquy is not a spiritual tool that I use every day. As a basic rule of thumb, I tend to use it on days when I finish meditation and still have some time left for prayer. As such, I do the colloquy for five to ten minutes and then end personal prayer by reviewing the prayer time and making some notes in my prayer journal about my desire, the object of my meditation, what stirred in my heart, and what I felt like God revealed.

Review the Prayer Time and then Journal

Because important moments are often recorded so that we can go back and savor them, Matt was able to show me the video on his iPhone of Sandy showing her engagement ring to her parents. He did a great job capturing their excitement and joy! In a world where almost everyone has a camera and video camera on their mobile phone, we are used to recording life's important events. While we usually record secular events with a camera, video camera, or a diary, we typically record prayer events with a prayer journal.

Ignatius recommended that we end our personal prayer time by reviewing what we prayed about and what we experienced, and then journal about it. We ask ourselves questions like "What happened during prayer?" "What feelings did I experience?" "What was God like?" and "What Scripture verse or other object of meditation did I use, and how did God speak to me through it?"

Despite the fact that writing in our prayer journal every day can bear tremendous spiritual fruit, such as revealing what God desires to show us and providing a record of how God is working in our lives, many people struggle to develop the habit. I have found that most of my new directees spend six months to a year developing the habit of journaling daily. Often, their struggle with journaling is rooted in the false expectation that they need to write multiple paragraphs. I explain to them that writing only a few sentences each day is often sufficient for helping us to remember the ongoing conversation we're having with God.

There are a couple of additional blessings to keeping a prayer journal. For those of you who are in spiritual direction, your journal can be a great way to prepare to meet with your spiritual director each month. In fact, I recommend that directees spend one or two prayer periods before their spiritual direction session simply reviewing the things they wrote in their journal, making notes about particular experiences of consolation or desolation or themes that emerged throughout the month. The prayer journal can also be used during spiritual direction sessions to make notes about new insights or important movements of the heart.

Undoubtedly, one of the most powerful deterrents to journaling is the fear that someone might read our prayer journal. In order for the journal to be fully beneficial, it's essential that we feel completely safe to write anything and everything in it, without filtering it for other people's viewing. Digital journals, such as a file on a laptop or a journal app on a smart tablet, now offer new levels of privacy and security. Many directees have found them to be precisely what they needed to move beyond their fear of being honest and open. Also, keeping a digital journal offers the possibility of saving pictures and videos we used for prayer, as well as easily copying and pasting various Scripture verses and spiritual quotes.

A Personal Example of Relational Prayer

Early in the morning on January 1, I lumbered out of bed, stopped briefly at the Keurig for a cup of hot coffee, and plopped down in my prayer chair. Using the structure for relational prayer that I just detailed in this chapter, I started my personal prayer time. I took about a minute to remember that the God of the universe is madly in love with me and is always present with me. Then I turned on the iPad and opened my prayer journal to the previous day's entry. As I did, I realized that it was the beginning of a new year and I spent some time reflecting on what the previous year had meant to me and feeling excited about the beginning of a new year.

I asked God for the grace to name my hopes and fears for the new year. Turning to one of the quintessential Scripture passages about new beginnings in Isaiah, I read—

> Remember not the events of the past,
> the things of long ago consider not;
> See, I am doing something new!
> Now it springs forth, do you not perceive it?
> In the wilderness I make a way,
> in the wasteland, rivers. ISAIAH 43:18–19

I shared with God my gratitude for specific blessings that I received the previous year, and then I shared my hopes and fears about the new year. I named the graces and virtues that I felt I would need in order to grow in faith, hope, and love throughout the upcoming months. Then I went back to the Scripture passage in Isaiah and let God remind me of his hope and blessings for me in the upcoming year.

After meditating on the Scripture, I was reminded of the new beginning Mary experienced when the angel Gabriel announced to her that she would conceive and bear a Son. I spent a few minutes talking to Mary about what I was feeling about the new year and what she felt at the angel's announcement. I compared our experiences, noting the similarities and differences.

I ended by reviewing my prayer time and journaling. As I did, a new insight surfaced in my consciousness; it moved me to tears. In my journal, I wrote—

> What's interesting, Father, is that my heart was filled with the
> most joy and hope while I journaled about the ways in which

I desire to bless *You* next year rather than how I hope *You* will bless *me*! Wow, I didn't expect that. I love You so much and desire for my life to be a blessing to You! Thank You for the mutuality of our love—for choosing me and accepting me and loving me, as I am, despite my faults, and for letting me serve You!

The fruit of my prayer time was a deeper appreciation of God's mutual love and my desire to serve him. What a beautiful gift! It was a special consolation, one that I continue to go back to frequently. I firmly believe that the structure of relational prayer that I offer in this chapter can help us to deeply and intimately connect with God. This is the intimacy I desire! This is the intimacy you desire!

REFLECTION QUESTIONS

1. Did you ever "nest" in preparation to bring a newborn child into your home? How did you prepare the baby's room? What made that preparation special? Have you "nested" for God? How have you prepared a special place for you and God to spend time together in prayer? What makes that sacred space special to you?

2. What is your heart's deepest desire at this moment in your life? In other words, if you could only talk with Jesus for fifteen minutes and it couldn't be intercessory prayer for others, what would you talk to him about?

3.   Have you ever used a prayer journal? If so, what was the experience like? If not, what hopes and fears do you feel regarding the use of one?

4.   Have you ever had a conversation with someone who has died (a saint or family member) as part of your personal prayer time? If so, what did you gain from the experience?

5.   What did you find the most helpful about this chapter? Why?

Java with Jesus

The intimacy that you and I desire to have with God is nurtured and cultivated through relational, personal prayer, which is something similar to meeting a close friend for coffee. It would be absurd to meet a friend at the local coffee shop and tell him what we need him to do for us or refuse to talk to him because "he already knows everything anyway." Instead, we would cherish the time we had with him and use it to share the most important things that were on our heart.

The conversation would be a dialogue, not a monologue. It would flow casually as we shared what is important to us and listened to our friend share similar experiences or offer us words of encouragement or challenge. We would not have expectations of him fixing anything in our life but would simply enjoy being present with him. The same thing is true in our relationship with God. When we allow personal prayer to be as relational as meeting our best friend at a coffee shop, then we experience new and deeper levels of mutuality and intimacy.

I hope this book has offered encouragement and ideas about how to make your personal prayer more relational, as well as revealed the marks of a healthy, intimate relationship with God that can help you better discern how God is inviting you into greater mutuality. Maybe it has given you a new freedom to ask important and discerning questions about your conversations with God, such as, "Would I say this to my best friend while we share a cup of coffee?"

As I conclude this book, I'm aware that none of the words I wrote can compare with you spending a few minutes in intimate personal prayer with God. The two are as different and unequal as a *travel book* about Ireland and an *actual trip* to Ireland. Sadly, many people settle for reading a bunch of travel books but never make the journey. Even sadder are those who read countless books about prayer but never make the spiritual journey of regularly spending time in relational and intimate personal prayer. Therefore, let us pray.

Creative Ideas for Relational Prayer

The following suggestions for personal prayer are in no way comprehensive. I have simply taken some of the most common spiritual desires that directees have shared with me and provided Scripture passages and meditation ideas for each one. The list is meant to stir up your own creativity regarding the topic of prayer that is most important to you and God right now. Many of the meditation suggestions can be easily adaptable to almost any grace or desire and can be lumped together into just a few basic approaches such as—use Scripture stories and verses, utilize your past memories and experiences, search the internet for articles, lists, and images, ask evocative questions, and find spiritual reading that corresponds to the grace you desire.

I have purposely made multiple recommendations for each grace as a way of reminding us that our topics of conversation with God do not change quickly but are pervasive for days, weeks, and even months. Therefore, we will need to use multiple Scripture passages and objects of meditation in order to continue the conversation with God about that particular topic or desire.

I begin each suggestion with the grace or desire written in the form of a prayer such as we would inscribe in our prayer journal. Then, I list a few Scriptures that can help us in our conversation with God about that desire. Finally, I offer some creative suggestions for how we can continue the conversation with God. As you'll notice, some of the suggestions entail things we would do *outside* of our personal prayer time and reflect on the next day in prayer. I hope you find these creative ideas for relational prayer helpful.

I desire to...

LOVE MORE DEEPLY

- Reflect on Scripture passages about love.

    I CORINTHIANS 13:4–8A *(replace the word "love" with your own name)* » I JOHN 4:7–21 » JOHN 15:9–17

- Since "God is love" and we are made "in the image and likeness" of God, then our deepest identity is love. Spend some time in prayer meditating on when you reflected love for others yesterday. When were you an incarnation of love?

- Google "qualities of love" and spend time reflecting on which ones stir up fear, hope, and gratitude.

- Think of the person you find the hardest to love and the person you find the easiest to love. What qualities about each of these people make it hard or easy to love them? What would God need to change in you to love both equally?

I desire to...
FOLLOW CHRIST MORE FAITHFULLY

- Reflect on Scripture stories of people leaving everything to follow Jesus.

  LUKE 6:12–16 *(the call of the Apostles)* » LUKE 5:1–11 *(the call of Peter)* » MATTHEW 9:9–13 *(the call of Matthew)*

- Share with God the ways in which you are faithfully following Christ and the ways you feel like you're struggling. What are the commonalities and differences between the two?

- Name the most faithful Christian you know, and share with God what you love most about that person.

- Search the internet for the "Kingdom Exercise" in the *Spiritual Exercises* and use it for meditation.

I desire to...
BE MORE LIKE JESUS

- Reflect on Scripture passages about Jesus.

  JOHN 12:20–36 » MATTHEW 16:13–28
  PHILIPPIANS 2:5–11

- Search the internet for the most important qualities of Christ and spend time sharing with Jesus which of those qualities you find within yourself and which ones you need.

- Read an entire gospel, spending time with just one story each day. Read the stories with one objective—to create a detailed description of the characteristics and values of Christ. Then, throughout each day, put that characteristic or value into action.

- Use small sections of a book like *To Know Christ Jesus* by Frank Sheed to learn more about Jesus. Then, talk to Christ about what you're learning about him.

I desire to...

SEE AND LOVE MYSELF
AS GOD SEES AND LOVES ME

- Reflect on Scripture passages that reaffirm the gift of who you are.

  ISAIAH 43:1–5 *(insert your name so that these are God's words to you)* » ISAIAH 62:2–5 » MARK 1:9–11 *(let yourself be in Jesus' place, hearing the Father's words)* » PSALM 139

- Share with God what you most love about yourself and what you most dislike about yourself. Then, ask God to share his opinion with you.

- Each day during prayer, let God thank you for five specific things you did or said the previous day. Let yourself deeply receive God's gratitude and appreciation for you.

- Ask your family members and friends to share with you what they love most about you, and then talk to God in prayer about their answers.

I desire to...

FORGIVE

- Reflect on Scripture passages on forgiveness.

  EPHESIANS 4:25–32 » **LUKE 15:11–32**

  COLOSSIANS 3:12–17

- In your prayer journal, make a list of the people you need to forgive and what they did to you. Share your list with God and ask for his perspective on who those people are and what they did.

- Using the story of the prodigal son, imagine each of the people who have hurt you returning to the Father. Share with the Father your response to their sorrow.

- Use a book like *Be Healed* by Bob Schuchts to better understand the grudges and resentments that you are holding onto and bring them to prayer.

- Share with Jesus your understanding of the difference between forgiveness and reconciliation and then research it on the internet. Take what you learn back to prayer.

I desire to...

TRUST GOD

- Reflect on Scripture stories about trust and dependence on God.

  MATTHEW 6:25–34 » **JOSHUA 21:43–45**

  PROVERBS 3:1–6

- Share with God your understanding of the difference between trusting that God will do what you want him to do and trusting that he will be with you no matter what happens.

- Research the difference between trust and faith and talk to God about it.

- Recall a time when God trusted you (or entrusted something/someone to you). What happens in your heart as you remember his trust? How did you respond to his trust?

- Share with God a time he let you down. Journal what happened and how it made you feel. Take time to let God show you where he was during that time.

I desire to...

EXPERIENCE GOD AS MY BELOVED

- Reflect on Scripture passages that offer images of God as our lover.

    SONG OF SONGS *(aka Song of Solomon)*

    HOSEA 2:16–25 » ISAIAH 62:2–5

- Choose a special way to express love toward God each day— pray about it and do it. Reflect on it the next morning.

- Read Dr. Gary Chapman's book *The Five Love Languages*, and reflect on how God speaks your unique love language and how you speak God's love language.

- Do a word search and study on the three Greek words for "love" in the New Testament—*philos*, *eros*, and *agape*—and apply them to your relationship with God (e.g., John 21).

- Plan a date night with God! Reflect on what it was like during your next prayer time.

I desire to...
GROW IN HUMILITY

- Reflect on Scripture passages about humility.

    PHILIPPIANS 2:5–11 » JAMES 3:13–18 » 1 PETER 5:5–11

- Beg God to humiliate you at least one time each day and then meditate on the experience the next morning in prayer.

- Search the internet for an image of humility that speaks to your heart. Meditate on it and talk to God about *why* and *what* it speaks to your heart.

- Share with God a personally humiliating memory. What is one positive gift that came from the experience?

I desire...
PEACE

- Reflect on Scripture verses about peace.

    COLOSSIANS 3:12–17 » JOHN 14:25–31 » LUKE 24:36–53

- Use sections of the book *Searching for and Maintaining Peace* by Jacques Philippe as conversation starters with Christ about the gift of peace.

- Reflect on the "Prayer of St. Francis" and share with God which parts are the easiest to pray and which ones are the hardest.

- Share with God a moment in your life when you felt the most peace. What did the peace feel like? How did God seem present in it?

I desire...

PATIENCE

- Reflect on Scripture passages about patience.
  ROMANS 5:3–8 » JAMES 1:2–4 » ROMANS 12:9–12

- Ask God to provide numerous opportunities each day to have your patience tried and then reflect on the experiences the next day in prayer. Which situations tried your patience the most?

- Share with God the one person who most frequently tries your patience. What characteristic about that person robs you of your patience? Why?

- The Hebrew language has a word that can be translated both "wait" and "hope." This word in the Old Testament is קוה (pronounced kaw-vaw') and can be found in numerous places, including in Psalm 130, which reads, "I wait for the LORD, my soul waits and I hope for his word" (130:5). Share with God how patience has helped you to both wait and hope.

I desire to...
BE MORE GRATEFUL

- Reflect on Scripture passages about gratitude.

  HEBREWS 12:14–29 » LUKE 17:11–19
  COLOSSIANS 3:12–17

- Learn about the Hebrew "*Dayenu*" prayer that is sung during Passover, and write your own.

- Use a "Gratitude Journal" app to grow in the practice of gratitude, moving beyond the obvious gifts.

- Study the "Psalms of Gratitude," naming the common responses to God's gifts that are found in them. What are your common responses to God's gifts? How do you express gratitude?

I desire to...
BE MORE SELFLESS

- Reflect on Scripture passages about selflessness.

  JOHN 15:9–17 » LUKE 6:37–38
  2 CORINTHIANS 9:10–15

- Meditate on five mysteries of the Rosary that reflect selflessness.

- Do a colloquy with a saint whom you know to be very generous. Find out the motivation and inspiration for his or her selflessness.

- Choose to do one random selfless act of kindness each day

and then share with God what the experience was like—the challenges and joys.

I desire to...
BE MORE GENTLE

- Reflect on Scripture passages about gentleness.

    GALATIANS 5:16–23 » JAMES 3:13–18 » JOHN 8:1–11

- Read small sections of a book on gentleness, such as *Spirituality and the Gentle Life* (Adrian Van Kaam) and meditate on it.

- Share with God what it means to be gentle with yourself, others, and creation.

- Share with God one moment yesterday when you were willful. What were the consequences? What would have been different had you been gentle?

I desire to...
BE MORE ACCEPTING

- Reflect on Scripture passages about accepting others and accepting situations.

    JOB 1:20–22 » JONAH 4:1–11

    LUKE 10:1–9 *(accepting what is offered to us)*

- Use sections of the book *Interior Freedom* by Jacques Philippe as conversation starters with Christ about acceptance.

- Beg God each morning to put people and situations in your

path that will annoy you, and then beg God for the grace to accept each of those annoyances as gifts from him.

- Remember someone you know who epitomizes acceptance of others and situations—someone who is joyful regardless—and share with God the qualities and characteristics about that person that you most love.

I desire to...
BE LESS JUDGMENTAL

- Reflect on Scripture passages about the importance of not judging.

   LUKE 6:37–42 » JAMES 4:7–12 » JOHN 7:14–24

- Share with God a time when you felt very judged by a family member, friend, or coworker. How did you respond? How did his or her judgment impact your view of yourself?

- Name the person (or group) with whom you are the most judgmental. Ask God for the grace to see him or her through the eyes of God.

I desire to...
LISTEN TO GOD

- Reflect on Scripture stories about the gift of listening.

   1 KINGS 19:9–13 » JAMES 1:19 » ECCLESIASTES 7:1–5

- Consciously listen for God's voice in the voices of the people whom you listen to today and reflect on it in prayer tomorrow. What did you hear God say through them?

- Spend time in contemplative prayer, being receptive to any thought or feeling that comes.

- Sit outside and deeply listen. Talk to God about what you hear and what you don't hear.

I desire to...
BE MORE GENEROUS

- Reflect on Scripture passages about generosity.

  2 CORINTHIANS 9:1–15 » LUKE 8:4–8 *(generosity of the sower)*
  JOHN 15:9–17

- Choose a different generous act to do each day—such as paying for the meal for the car behind you in the drive-thru—and then meditate with God on the experience the next day in personal prayer.

- Name the people with whom you find it easiest to be generous, as well as the ones with whom you find it the hardest. What are the commonalities within these two groups?

- Share with God a time when another human being was extremely generous with you. What affective movements did it stir up in your heart? Why?

I desire...

WISDOM

- Reflect on Scripture verses about the gift of wisdom.

  1 KINGS 3:1–15 » ISAIAH 11:1–4 » 1 CORINTHIANS 2:6–16

- Think of someone you know who possesses wisdom. What exactly makes him or her wise? How is his or her wisdom manifested?

- Research the differences between wisdom, knowledge, and understanding. Share with God your findings.

- Write in your prayer journal about a time when you experienced the gift of wisdom at work within you.

I desire to...

BE JOYFUL

- Reflect on Scripture passages about joy and rejoicing.

  PHILIPPIANS 4:4 » LUKE 10:17–20 » 1 PETER 4:12–14

- Look for an opportunity to be joyful, either in word or deed, and reflect on the experience during prayer.

- Search the internet for images of joy and meditate on the one that most deeply touches your heart. Share with God why it touches your heart.

- Reflect on a time in your life when you felt overjoyed. How was God present to you at that moment? What image of God most accurately portrays who he was for you?

I desire to...
BE HONEST

- Reflect on Scripture verses about being honest.

  EPHESIANS 4:25 » MATTHEW 5:37 » JOHN 14:6

- Ask God to share with you the various qualities necessary for honesty, such as humility. Which of those qualities do you already see present in yourself?

- Share with God a time when you told a lie that led to more lies. What was the experience like and how did God draw you back into the truth?

- Make a habit of immediately apologizing for any lie or embellishment that you tell, and then reflect on the experience in personal prayer.

I desire to...
BE HEALED

- Reflect on Scripture passages on spiritual and physical healing.

  MARK 10:46–52 » LUKE 5:17–26 » MATTHEW 9:18–26

- Share with God the healing you most deeply desire and why you desire it.

- Meditate on Saint Ignatius of Loyola's "Principle and Foundation" as paraphrased by David Fleming, SJ (see pages 14–15), and share with God what stirs in your heart as you read the description of being unbiased.

- When have you seen or experienced God's healing? How did it affect you or others?

I desire to...
GROW IN FREEDOM

- Reflect on Scripture passages about the freedom God desires for us.

  GALATIANS 5:13–23 » ROMANS 8:18–21
  2 CORINTHIANS 3:17–18

- Use sections of the book *Interior Freedom* by Jacques Philippe as conversation starters with Christ about freedom.

- Reflect on a time in your life when you felt the freest. Did it feel more like a "freedom from" or a "freedom for"? Why?

- What image or symbol of freedom most deeply touches your heart? Why?

I desire to...
HAVE HOLY INDIFFERENCE

- Reflect on Scripture verses about acceptance of God's will and all circumstances.

  JOB 1:21 » GENESIS 22:1–18 » ROMANS 8:28–31

- Share with God the people or things that you are most attached to and the importance those attachments have had in your life.

- Talk to Jesus about the differences between detachment and apathy.

- Sacrificially fast from something you're attached to and then share the experience with God.

I desire to...

EMBODY THE BEATITUDES

- Reflect on Scripture passages.

  ISAIAH 55:8–9 *(God's ways are different than we would expect)*
  MATTHEW 5:1–12 » LUKE 6:20–26

- Share with God several examples of what each Beatitude would look like if you put it into action.

- Which Beatitudes stir up the most fear or the most peace?

- Spend time meditating on the level of intimacy required by the Beatitudes versus the Ten Commandments.